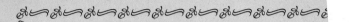

Daily Devotions

for Seniors

Scriptures, Readings,
Prayers, and More

CHRISTINE A. DALLMAN

PUBLICATIONS INTERNATIONAL, LTD.

Christine A. Dallman is a freelance writer living in the Seattle area. She has contributed to the devotional publication, *The Quiet Hour*, and is a former editor and columnist for *Sunday Digest* magazine.

Louis Weber, CEO
Publications International, Ltd.
7373 North Cicero Avenue
Lincolnwood, Illinois 60712

Manufactured in U.S.A.

8 7 6 5 4 3 2 1

ISBN: 0-7853-3486-6

CONTENTS

INTRODUCTION

~⊙~

*A*S A SENIOR, you represent a group of people that has played a vital role in the development of at least one, and perhaps two or three, generations. It is your own strength that has filled the pages of this book with invaluable themes. This book is an echo of your life, coming back to you as a reminder of the power of your life, whether through spiritual strength, your kind ways, your gentle touch, your enduring love, or your words of praise. Each meditation has been written in hope that you will gain inner strength from its uplifting message.

These devotionals include a verse of Scripture, a theme, and a thought for the day, followed by a brief prayer. The range of topics includes love, peace, personal growth, faith, humor, and wisdom, just to name a few. Take a moment each day to nurture your soul with the encouraging words from these pages, and in doing so, experience the freshness of a renewed outlook.

COMPASSION
COMPASSION FOR OTHERS

. . . .

GRANDPARENTS: COMPASSION IN PERSON

The compassion of grandparents is a refuge for grandchildren.

Verse for the Day: "My child, give me your heart, and let your eyes observe my ways" (Prov 23:26).

RAISED IN A STRICT HOME, Angela was very familiar with the cause-and-effect relationship between bad behavior and discipline. Her place of refuge was at Grandma's house.

Grandma seldom chided, and she knew how to make light of shortcomings. Kindness and compassion abounded at Grandma's house. If something got broken, there were no harsh words about carelessness. When siblings bickered, Grandma could understand each point of view and find a solution. If Angela was bored, Grandma stopped to play a game, take a walk, or explore in the big yard.

For many children, grandparents are their first look at compassion. Kids can experience a safety zone of unconditional acceptance and understanding as their grandmas and grandpas ease the embarrassment of mistakes and absolve the guilt of wrongs. And as compassion is modeled for them, they learn, in turn, to extend compassion to those around them.

Prayer: Thank you, God, that your compassion can flow through me to my grandchildren.

* * * *

REMEMBERING WHAT IT WAS LIKE

Remembering our own awkward years gives us compassion for the young.

~✥~

Verse for the Day: "Bear with one another" (Col 3:13).

IN A SMALL TOWN, three young boys hurried into the general store and crowded the sales counter. "How can I help you?" asked the elderly store owner.

One of the boys pointed to a display of fishing tackle high up on the wall behind the store owner. "I'd like two dollars' worth of fishing hooks," he quickly said.

The owner went to the aisle in which he'd been working and brought back his small stepladder. With some difficulty, he climbed the ladder and brought down a box of hooks from the shelf. After counting out the right amount, he put them in a bag and returned the box to its place. He then turned to the next boy and asked, "Is there anything I can do for you, Brian?"

"I'll have two dollars' worth of fishhooks, too."

Obviously annoyed, he said, "It would have been better if you'd told me sooner!" Nevertheless, he climbed the ladder again, retrieved the box of hooks, and filled the order. Then before putting the box of hooks back, he asked the third boy, "John, do you want two dollars' worth of fishhooks, too?"

"No," came a quiet reply.

So the owner climbed the ladder once again and returned the box. When he came back to the boys, a little out of breath, he smiled at John and asked, "What do you want, John?"

"A dollar's worth of fishhooks."

The foolishness of youth. Sometimes it's humorous, sometimes maddening. But in dealing with children, it helps to remember what it was like to be young.

In fact, children find comfort and refuge in the encouragement and warmth of a grandparent's smile. They respond to the empathy of a compassionate presence in their world of questions and discovery. Grandparents are a much-needed ally in the hurry-up, no-nonsense atmosphere of grown-up life.

Prayer: God, it's a privilege to be a gentle presence in the lives of the children I encounter.

* * * *

Mrs. Trapp's Tenderness

Tenderness toward others can change them in a way that force cannot.

~◈~

Verse for the Day: "Finally, all of you, have . . . sympathy, love for one another, a tender heart, and a humble mind" (1 Pet 3:8).

LESLIE WAS A POUTING, selfish brat, as I recall from kindergarten days. At least, she started out that way. No one, absolutely no one, wanted to be her friend within the first week of school.

I don't know how long Mrs. Trapp had taught, but she was well into her sixties when I was her student. And she was as patient an educator as I would ever meet.

Each morning, Mrs. Trapp would select a new VIP for the day. That student chose a helper to unfold the flag and lead the class in the "Pledge of Allegiance." The VIP also was commissioned to take his or her partner down to the cafeteria's kitchen to carry up trays of cookies and milk for snack time. It was a coveted honor, and the VIP always chose his or her best friend as a helper.

When my day to be VIP came around for the second time that year, I was fully prepared to select my partner. But before I could, Mrs. Trapp took me aside and whispered something utterly unimaginable in my ear. "Will you pick Leslie?" she asked.

"Why?" I asked incredulously. Her answer came with a pleading look of concern: "Leslie needs a friend." I understood, but it was still painful to call out, "Today I choose Leslie as my partner."

Mrs. Trapp's mission to melt Leslie's hostility was underway. First, Leslie looked around in disbelief, but because everyone was looking back at her, she realized that she had heard correctly. "Me?" she squealed and bounded to the front of the room to stand with me.

As the day progressed, I noticed that Leslie was trying hard to be nice. Mrs. Trapp's plan was already taking effect. I'd like to say it was an overnight success, but it wasn't. It took many weeks before Leslie established friendships with some of us. By the time the year was over, however, she was one of us.

Last I heard, Mrs. Trapp, now in her nineties, was recently honored at a special celebration for her many years of service in education. Though I learned my ABCs from her, I'll always remember her more for the TLC she gave to all of us.

Prayer: God, wherever I encounter hostility, let the tenderness of my compassion disarm it.

* * * *

COMPASSION FOR THE SUFFERING IN THE WORLD

* * * *

DISCREET COMPASSION

Sometimes the way in which we give is as much an act of compassion as the gift itself.

~⚭~

Verse for the Day: "[Jesus] stretched out his hand and touched [the leper], saying '. . . Be made clean!' Immediately his leprosy was cleansed" (Matt 8:3).

FRENCH ACTRESS SARAH BERNHARDT enjoyed great fame until her death in 1923 at nearly 80 years of age. She was also a person of compassion.

An old issue of *Ladies Home Journal* carried the following account about her as related by Elsie de Wolfe:

"A bowl stood on a secluded hall table at the home of Sarah Bernhardt, and one day I noticed that a few of her guests, in leaving, after looking around to make sure they were unnoticed, slipped something from it into their pockets. I asked about it, and Sarah explained that, as many of her friends were in need, she kept the bowl filled with coins. 'They know it is there, and for what purpose,' she said. 'In this way, I can help them without putting them to the necessity of asking for it.'"

Within this gesture of kindness were actually two compassionate acts: the first being the monetary gifts and the second being the discreet way in which they were made available, graciously sparing her friends' dignity.

Whenever we give in a way that helps others maintain their sense of worth and dignity, the gift we give is more than doubled in value. For though compassion is costly, human dignity is priceless.

Prayer: Dear God, impart your sensitivity to me when I give to those in need.

❦ ❦ ❦ ❦

Simple Acts of Compassion

**Some of the noblest acts we will ever
do are simple acts of compassion.**

*Verse for the Day: "Go and learn what this means,
'I desire mercy, not sacrifice'"* (Matt 9:13).

WHEN THE RELIGIOUS LEADERS of Jesus' day were wrapped up in making a reputation for themselves as pious, noble, and righteous, Jesus challenged them to revamp their thinking. "Go and learn what this means," he told them, "'I desire mercy, not sacrifice.'"

In God's, eyes our most noble deeds are not necessarily the things the world considers awe-inspiring. A missionary once said there are at least two reasons people fail to exercise compassion: (1) we long to do the really big, brave, noble things that are beyond our reach; or (2) we may refuse to render service that seems insignificant or beneath our dignity.

We look at martyrs, missionaries, and saints with an eye of admiration, and we regard them with honor and esteem. In fact, their noble acts have earned them a place in humanity's hall of fame. Nevertheless, what does living more nobly translate into for the average person?

Each time we take an opportunity to extend help to a needy neighbor, a listening ear to someone who's hurting, groceries to a local food bank, our time to a nearby charitable organization, or a visit or phone conversation to a lonely individual, we have acted nobly.

It is these simple acts of compassion, not our grand demonstrations of sacrifice, that please God most and effectively hold together the fabric of humanity.

Prayer: God, as those who need compassion come my way, may I remember that mercy is the desire of your heart.

* * *

ONE NEED AT A TIME
**Each time we administer compassion,
we help alleviate the world's suffering.**

Verse for the Day: "Bear one another's burdens, and in this way you will fulfill the law of Christ" (Gal 6:2).

DARLENE AND BRIAN had been attending services at a community church for several months. Finally, they disclosed that Darlene had been struggling with a drug addiction and wanted to break free from it. They asked for the church's prayers.

As Darlene made the tough decision to enter a drug-treatment facility, the church community rallied around the young family. People from the congregation attended a special meeting called to plan child care and meals that would carry the couple through the time Darlene would be absent from her home for treatment.

Today, Darlene is drug-free, and she and Brian have felt their burden of suffering lifted. Now they participate in a loving church community that is reaching out to those who are hurting.

It's inspiring to see compassion at work, saving people's lives and helping them get on their feet. Although the world is full of suffering and our efforts on a global scale seem minuscule, we can take heart. It was Mother Teresa's example that reminded people everywhere that the work of compassion can happen effectively only as we embrace the needs of others—one needy person at a time.

Each need met—each suffering heart that finds relief in our love—is one more person who becomes free to join in the crusade of compassion that is quietly changing our world.

Prayer: Continue to free others from their suffering, God, through my compassion for them.

＊　＊　＊　＊

TRUE COMPASSION
My acts of charity to assist the suffering
demonstrate the depth of my compassion.

Verse for the Day: "*A Samaritan while traveling came near
him; and when he saw him, he was moved with pity. He went
to him and bandaged his wounds, having poured oil and
wine on them. Then he put him on his own animal, brought
him to an inn, and took care of him*" (Luke 10:33–34).

LATE ONE AFTERNOON, a wealthy CEO stepped out
of his downtown office building and into the
subzero temperatures of the Midwest. Hurrying to
his waiting ride, he shivered as the gusts of wind cut
through his overcoat. When the car door had closed
behind him and he had settled into the comfortable
warmth inside, he made a note to himself to have
an administrative assistant arrange delivery of wool
blankets and warm clothing to local homeless
shelters.

The next day at the office, as he checked his calendar
and memos he'd made to himself, the CEO came across
the note about the clothing and blankets. *It's not as cold
today,* he thought. "And I just don't have time to deal
with this right now," he mumbled, crossing it off of his
agenda. "Maybe later."

It's our acts, not our mere thoughts, of charity that reflect the depth of our concern for those in need. When we follow through on our benevolent intentions, we demonstate that the distresses and hardships of others really matter to us—that we truly care.

In contrast to the story above, the wealthy R. G. Letourneau used to give 90 percent of his business profits to charity and other worthy causes. He kept only 10 percent for himself. Of course, most of us couldn't survive on only 10 percent of our income, but we know that each charitable thought we've turned into action—however large or small—has made a difference in someone's struggle. Perhaps one day heaven will reveal to us just how far our gifts of compassion have gone toward alleviating the pain and hopelessness of others.

Prayer: God, grant me the wisdom and the means to give— whether time, finances, or otherwise—in ways that will truly help those in need.

* * * *

RECEIVING COMPASSION FROM OTHERS

. . . .

COMPASSION FROM GOD

Receiving God's compassion for us transforms our lives.

Verse for the Day: "But you, O Lord, are a God merciful and gracious, slow to anger and abounding in steadfast love and faithfulness. . . . you, Lord, have helped me and comforted me" (Psa 86:15, 17).

THERE IS AN OPAL some call the "sympathetic jewel." On its own it is lusterless, but when a hand rubs it, a wonderful change occurs in its appearance. The opal comes alive with a spectrum of gleaming colors.

A parallel exists between this illustration and our relationship with God. When we live apart from God's love, we lack a certain aliveness. It's not until we permit God to hold us in his hand that we find ourselves coming to life in a way we had not experienced before. And only then is our countenance transformed, revealing all the colors of our potential and purpose.

Prayer: God, let all the colors of my life shine in your hand.

. . . .

When Compassion Comes Our Way

**Compassion, once received,
can be passed freely along to others.**

*Verse for the Day: "You received without payment;
give without payment"* (Matt 10:8).

*I*N THE SUPERMARKET checkout line, customers
waited behind a woman whose groceries had been
rung up. Finding herself a dollar or so short for her
purchases, she debated whether she should hurry to
her car and retrieve some change. Instead, she began to
select items she could do without, intending to have
them subtracted from the total bill.

As she put aside the few things she planned to leave
behind, another customer reached out and handed her
a five-dollar bill. "Oh, no, that's OK," the embarrassed
woman said. "I can always come back."

"Please take it," the customer insisted. "Others have
done the same for me in the past."

Giving in with a smile of gratitude, the woman took
the money and said, "I'll be sure to pass along the
kindness again to someone else."

"That's just what it's for," said the other shopper.

Seeing gifts as something to be passed on rather than a debt to be repaid is a wonderful way to extend the gifts of compassion and kindness. In fact, in remembrance of what we have received, we can multiply the gift by passing it along to whomever we can.

Prayer: God, give me grace to receive the compassion of others when I need it and the opportunity to pass it along.

.   .   .

GIVING THROUGH RECEIVING

Receiving compassion from another person helps both of us.

Verse for the Day: "Two are better than one . . . For if they fall, one will lift up the other" (Eccl 4:9–10).

CASANDRA WAS MOVING into a new apartment. She hoped to be able to do most of the work herself but knew she would need help with the larger furniture. Friends and family offered their assistance to lighten the load, but she would accept help only on limited terms. "I'll just need help with the big stuff," she told her dad and waved off everyone else with a polite "thanks, but no thanks."

When moving day arrived, Casandra found herself having completed only part of what she had wanted to get done. She had been unrealistic about the time she had available to work on packing. Reluctantly she solicited her mom's help as well, and (rather than the work party she might have had to complete the task in short order) she and her parents spent the entire day getting everything moved in.

It's human nature to want to fend for ourselves. We hate to accept offers of help, and we hate to ask for help. Often it takes laying down our pride to receive the compassion others extend. If, however, we will keep in mind a little reciprocity principle that governs giving and receiving, it helps us have a better perspective.

Throughout our lives, we've heard that it's more of a blessing to give than to receive, and that is true. It is also true that a willingness to receive compassion from those around us can be a gift to them as well. How can that be? Think about the last time you wanted to help a friend, and he or she took you up on your offer. It likely made you feel good, trusted, and needed. You probably received a lot of gratitude in return. You gave, but you also received a great deal back.

Prayer: God, grant me the grace to receive compassion so that those who give it may be blessed as well.

❧ ❧ ❧ ❧

CONTENTMENT
LEARNING TO BE CONTENT

. . . .

CONTENTMENT IN A CHANGING WORLD

Many things in life come and go, but our contentment can remain constant.

Verse for the Day: "[There is] a time to seek, and a time to lose; a time to keep, and a time to throw away" (Eccl 3:6).

THE PAST FEW GENERATIONS of seniors have seen more rapid changes in their lifetimes than other generations in human history. While the writer of Ecclesiastes asserted that nothing is ever really new, these generations of seniors might well retort, "Oh, yeah? If only something would stay the same!"

From horse-and-buggy to trains and motor cars, and from crop-dusters to rockets and space shuttles, the last century has been an explosion of technology. Entertainment, medicine, communication, education, transportation, the military—virtually every area of life has undergone dramatic change. Some changes have been for the better, such as new heart surgery techniques.

Other changes have questionable or even negative effects, such as the threat posed by nuclear weaponry. For better or worse, however, the externals of our lives continue changing at an overwhelming pace.

What can be done? The inevitability of it all precludes our protests. And if we long for a simpler time, we have only past memories as a retreat from the modern chaos. There is a way, however—whether we're young or old—to live in this present world without getting lost in the mad rush of change.

In a word, it is contentment. When we are at peace within ourselves, we can maintain contentment no matter how insane the world becomes. That's not to say we seek to establish a state of naïve bliss or that we ignore what goes on around us. Rather, our inner contentment is what gives us the strength to face the outside changes head-on, to take action when necessary, to embrace the good, and to decry the evil without becoming cynical.

Fads may come and gadgets may go, but contentment comes from a solid character. Indeed, one who has cultivated contentment will remain steady whatever else may change.

Prayer: God, thank you that my contentment is more solid than the world is shaky.

* * * *

FOCUSING ON THE GOOD

Contentment comes when we focus on the
good in life and in others.

*Verse for the Day: "[I]f there is any excellence
and if there is anything worthy of praise,
think about these things" (Phlp 4:8).*

THE LYRICS TO MORE THAN 8,500 hymns were born
in the mind of a woman named Fanny Crosby in
the nineteenth century. Many of them still remain
popular today.

Tragically, Fanny was robbed of her eyesight in infancy
when a man, who pretended to be a doctor, gave
Fanny's parents the wrong prescription for a cold. The
drug made her blind.

Nevertheless, when Fanny was well into her eighties,
having lived her life without being able to see, someone
asked her about her feelings toward this man. Without
hesitation, she affirmed that she did not, nor had she
ever, felt any kind of resentment toward him. Rather,
she saw her blindness as an opportunity to do the work
God had for her to do.

While she grew up, Fanny's parents had encouraged her
to be self-sufficient. She could dress herself, fix her hair,
climb trees, and ride horseback. And she loved to learn.

Her passion for poetry ran strong and deep. She attended New York Institute for the Blind, became a top-notch student, and went on to teach. By age 20, she had distinguished herself in New York, not as a scholar or teacher, but as an orator, who could deliver wonderful recitations of poetry.

As her faith in God grew, she let her skills loose on writing verse that could be set to the music of the church. Apparently, she could compose several complete hymns in her mind before having a secretary write them down. Song after song came forth, each reflecting her deepening belief in and love for God.

In her late thirties, Fanny met and married musician Alexander Van Alstyne, who was also blind. Together they had only one child who died as an infant. The couple shared one another's company during 44 years of marriage.

Fanny Crosby's later years saw her busy as ever. She remained optimistic and never complained, though she was faced with difficulties. Her soul always returned to a deep sense of contentment, for her inner sight always looked toward the good she found in life.

Prayer: God, give me the sight to see that the good things in my life outshine the bad.

* * * *

THE SECRET OF CONTENTMENT

**True contentment does
not depend on circumstances.**

*Verse for the Day: "I know what it is to have little, and
I know what it is to have plenty. In any and all circumstances
I have learned the secret of being well-fed and of going hungry,
of having plenty and of being in need"* (Phlp 4:12).

BY ALL OUTWARD APPEARANCES, Nathan has everything a person could possibly want to enjoy a
comfortable life. He is retired with his wife of 40 years,
owns a beautiful home in a nice neighborhood, drives a
luxury car, takes expensive vacations, and eats at the
best restaurants in town.

Ironically, however, Nathan is not content. He is impa-
tient and short-tempered with his wife. He complains
that his home is being devalued by the single-parent
neighbor who lives three houses down and who fails
to mow her lawn as often as Nathan feels she should.
While on vacations and in restaurants, he always
finds things to criticize about the food and service he
receives.

Meanwhile, across town Milton lives alone in a small,
one-bedroom rental home. It is all he can afford on his

meager pension. He uses public transportation, because his budget won't support the added burden of car insurance, fuel, and maintenance. Interestingly, people who know Milton describe him as friendly and delightful. He enjoys helping his neighbors with their yard work and is frequently invited to dinner in their homes.

Even in his enviable circumstances, Nathan is miserable because he has never learned what Milton discovered many years earlier: Contentment is not found outside one's self, but within. Milton will tell you that a person who complains in lowly circumstances will complain in good circumstances as well, while a person who has learned to look for the good in life, no matter what the situation, flourishes in happiness and contentedness.

Prayer: I'm glad, God, for the contentment that comes in knowing that no matter what the circumstances, you will always be with me and strengthen me when I need it.

*   *   *   *

AFFECTING OTHERS WITH OUR CONTENTMENT

. . . .

CONTENTMENT QUIETS COMPLAINING

Our spirit of contentment can help change complaining into positive attitudes and actions.

Verse for the Day: "Happy are those who do not follow the advice of the wicked, or take the path that sinners tread, or sit in the seat of scoffers" (Psa 1:1).

*S*TAN IS OPTIMISTIC BY NATURE and tends to see the positive possibilities in almost any situation. Yet his optimism is undergirded by a trait he has had to work to develop over the years—a trait that does not come naturally to any of us: contentment.

Watching Stan interact with his grandchildren, one can quickly see that he has become a master at quieting their discontented complaints. Amazingly, he doesn't accomplish this feat by shushing or shaming, but rather by guiding his grandchildren to a place where they can find contentment for themselves. Stan's guidance may take the form of helping a grandchild gain a new outlook on a circumstance, or it may come in the form of problem solving, that is, coming up with a constructive course of action that can help them initiate changes.

A scenario might go like this:

"I hate those girls!" granddaughter Julia complains.

"Why do you feel that way about them?" Stan asks.

"They're just jerks!" Julia answers.

"Tell me what happened to make you feel that way."

Then, while Julia senses her grandfather's concern, she calms down enough to tell him about a negative encounter in which she felt humiliated by a group of girls at school. After Stan listens and soothes her hurt feelings, he begins to help his granddaughter think through what happened and come up with a way to deal with her feelings and with future encounters with these antagonistic fellow students.

Under Stan's gentle influence, his grandchildren regain a sense that all is right with the world. While he guides them, they learn his secret of dealing with situations as situations, not allowing them to shake the solid ground of personal contentment.

Prayer: Lead me, God, as I lead others away from complaining toward real contentment.

* * * *

CAUSING CONTENTMENT IN OTHERS

My own contentment can be the cause of contentment in others.

Verse for the Day: "There is great gain in godliness combined with contentment" (1 Tim 6:6).

THE FAMILIAR ADAGE "Happiness can't be bought" seems ignored in our society, which measures success by the number of digits in one's salary. The wise, however, know that this adage is true. They know, too, that true happiness and contentment are much more attainable than a million-dollar salary. Every time we enjoy a sunset, every time we hold a child, every time we greet the morning with joy, we feed our souls and nourish our sense of contented happiness.

Yet the attainment of contentment is only half of the benefit. Unlike money, happiness costs us little to share. A smile, a sincere compliment, a hug, a listening ear— all can be catalysts for joy and contentment in others.

Prayer: God, you have made contentment readily available to me. Thank you that today I can welcome it and pass it along to others.

$ $ $ $

FAITH
AN ANCHOR FOR LIFE

• • • •

THE FLYING SCOTSMAN

Genuine faith guides our actions and decisions, and it pleases God.

Verse for the Day: "Without faith it is impossible to please God" (Heb 11:6).

THE 1981 FILM *CHARIOTS OF FIRE* portrayed the inspiring faith of a remarkable Scottish track star—Eric Liddell. Just three months before running in the 1923 AAA Championships held in London, the soft-spoken Liddell talked publicly about his faith in God for the first time. Eighty people gathered in a town hall in Armdale, Scotland, to hear Liddell's words. His quiet talk simply and clearly conveyed the strength he felt from knowing that God loved and cared for him.

The next morning, newspapers in Scotland carried the story of Liddell's "sermon." When he approached the starting line at the AAA Championships, word had spread about his faith, and many in England watched with interest as the man with a quiet trust in God won the 220- and 100-yard dashes. He was awarded the

Harvey Cup for the meet's best performance, and then he set his sights on the 1924 Paris Summer Olympics.

Once at the Olympics, Liddell learned that the heats in his best events were scheduled to be run on Sunday. Though shocked by the news, Liddell's convictions remained steadfast. He refused to run. He felt strongly that the day he had set aside to worship God should not take second place to his personal interests for glory.

He would settle for running in the 200- and 400-meter dashes, because qualifying heats for those races were scheduled for another day. On July 9, he won an unexpected bronze medal in the 200-meter sprint, and although he made his way through the heats for the 400-meter race, he was not a favorite to win.

The 400 would be Liddell's last race in the Olympic games. In his characteristic manner, Liddell shook hands with each of his competitors and then crouched at the starting line. When the gun went off, "The Flying Scotsman" ran with abandon in his unorthodox style with his face turned skyward. He finished five meters ahead of the second runner to cross the finish line, setting a then-world-record time of 47.6 seconds and winning a gold medal.

Eric Liddell won much more than an Olympic title that day; he won the respect of the world for his unswerving life of faith—a faith that determined the course he would run for the rest of his life until he died for his faith as a missionary in China.

Prayer: God, thank you for the gift of faith that guides me through each day.

* * * *

LINCOLN'S BIBLE

God's Word is a source of strength for a life of steadfast faith.

Verse for the Day: "The name of the Lord is a strong tower; the righteous run into it and are safe" (Prov 18:10).

A MODERN-DAY MINISTER once had the rare privilege of examining Abraham Lincoln's Bible. The pastor reverently held the old book in his hands while he pondered that it had first belonged to the president's mother, who had read from it to her son and had required him to memorize portions of its content.

Out of curiosity, the minister let the book fall open by itself to see what passage had been consulted most frequently. The Scripture that lay before him was Psalm 37: "Fret not thyself because of evil-doers. . . . Rest in the Lord, and wait patiently for him" (vss 1, 7). The page on which the passage appeared was worn from use. No doubt the president had turned to it again and again during the tumultuous era of his time in office.

Although the nature of Abraham Lincoln's faith in God has been debated, there is no doubt that God's Word had an indelible influence on the president's beliefs and actions. His penchant for forgiveness, his concern for all people, and his deep sense of acting justly all point to the principles he learned as a boy while his mother read to him from the Scriptures. And the tattered page on which Psalm 37 appears indicates that Lincoln had turned often to the Word of God to keep his faith strong and steady.

Prayer: God, I cherish your Word as it steadies my faith in an unsteady world.

* * * *

THE STRENGTH WE NEED
When we place our faith in God, he gives us his strength to meet life's challenges.

~⟨♡⟩~

Verse for the Day: "May you be made strong with all the strength that comes from his glorious power" (Col 1:11).

CHARLIE WAS A PARATROOPER in the Korean War and was decorated for valor when he saved the lives of his comrades during combat. After the war, Charlie married and had five children. He built his own home and provided faithfully for his family. Charlie was strong and could handle anything life threw at him.

"I was pretty self-sufficient," Charlie admits. "My wife had a strong faith in God, and that was fine with me, but I just didn't think I needed God in my life. But then something happened that made me realize there are things in life I can't control."

Charlie and his wife had raised their children and were looking forward to their retirement years when Charlie's wife suddenly became very ill. Charlie nursed her at home and found himself praying for the first time in a long time.

"I asked God to come into my life, forgive my pride and stubbornness, and give me strength," Charlie says. "And God did."

Charlie says he wonders why he had waited so long to invite God into his life to give him strength for living. He says it's not like the crutch some people describe, but it's like the best friend you'll ever have with you every minute of the day. It's a strength much greater than our human abilities, and it can handle anything— big or small—that comes our way.

Prayer: I place my trust in you, God, for strength in every situation I face.

* * * *

BELIEVING GOD'S PROMISES

* * * *

BELIEVING BEFORE SEEING

God's promises are trustworthy even when we can't see how he will accomplish them.

*Verse for the Day: "[F]or we walk by faith,
not by sight" (2 Cor 5:7).*

*A*FTER WORLD WAR II, the following words were found inscribed on a cellar wall in Germany: "I believe in the sun, / even when it is not shining; / I believe in love, / even when I feel it not / I believe in God, / even when He is silent." Such is the nature of faith—believing what we know to be true is still true even when everything we see seems contrary to it.

People of faith know God has not promised a life free of difficulty but rather to be with us in difficulty. King David wrote, "Even though I walk through the darkest valley, I fear no evil; for you are with me" (Psa 23:4).

We can believe God's promises regardless of immediate circumstances, for we know that God does not lie. "Whatever you ask for in prayer with faith," Jesus promised, "you will receive" (Matt 21:22).

A preacher once chided his congregation for their lack of faith. They had met to pray for rain to end a drought that was threatening crops. When he began the prayer meeting, he said sternly, "You know why we've come. What I want to know is, where are your umbrellas?"

The kind of faith that requests rain with an umbrella in hand is the kind of faith that pleases God. It is faith that knows the rain clouds are coming presently, though they are not yet visible on the horizon.

Prayer: God, I praise you because you are trustworthy.

✽ ✽ ✽

PROVIDING WHAT WE NEED

While we trust God, he will take care of our needs just as he has promised.

Verse for the Day: Jesus said, "Do not worry, saying, 'What will we eat?' or 'What will we drink?' or 'What will we wear?'... indeed your heavenly Father knows that you need all these things" (Matt 6:31–32).

M Y GRANDMA, a Depression-era child, has said from time to time what I've heard many say from that period of economic struggle: "We were poor, but I never knew it." Perhaps this is due to the fact that the basic necessities of life, though not in great abundance, were always enough to meet her family's needs as her parents depended on God's promise to provide.

Nevertheless, while they struggled through those lean years, they learned not to take God's provisions for granted. Even today, many who went through the Great Depression are not quick to discard food or possessions. After all, this is a generation who did not have the luxury of just throwing out clothing on a whim. They became survivors who found ways to make things last. So if anyone in our country today understands the adage "Waste not, want not," it is these seniors.

This combination of trust in God's goodness and an appreciation for all he provides has given this group a wonderful perspective on God's care for those who trust him. This generation knows that no matter how difficult life becomes, God will be true to his word and supply what we need. Also, as these seniors model for their children and grandchildren gratefulness for and careful management of God's bountiful blessings, they help remind younger generations that these provisions are from a loving God and need to be cherished.

Prayer: God, I trust you for everything that I need.

❦ ❦ ❦ ❦

Promises Defeat Doubt

Doubt is no match for the assurance
God's promises bring.

Verse for the Day: "When God desired to show even more clearly... the unchangeable character of his purpose, he guaranteed it by an oath, so that through two unchangeable things, in which it is impossible that God would prove false, we... might be strongly encouraged to seize the hope set before us" (Heb 6:17–18).

IN JOHN BUNYAN'S CLASSIC ALLEGORY *Pilgrim's Progress,* which he wrote from a prison cell, he relates an incident in which the main character, Christian, decides to take a detour off the Main Highway to follow another path that seems easier than the one he has been traveling. The alternate path, however, leads Christian into the regions where the Giant of Despair lives. The giant captures Christian and keeps him in the dungeon at Doubting Castle, where he advises Christian to end his life, telling him there is no use in continuing his journey to the Celestial City.

As the giant's words threaten to overwhelm Christian, his companion, Hopeful, who has also been captured, begins to remind Christian of the previous victories in their journey. With that bit of encouragement, the two begin to sing and pray, continuing all night until it is almost daybreak. Then, just before sunrise, Christian suddenly calls out, "What a fool am I thus to lie in a stinking Dungeon, when I may as well be at liberty. I have a Key in my bosom called Promise that will, I am persuaded, open any lock in Doubting Castle."

"That's good news," says Hopeful, who urges, "Good Brother, pluck it out of thy bosom and try." Much to their joy, the key called Promise indeed works, and both travelers go free and return to the Main Highway.

Bunyan's allegory closely parallels our journey of faith. Though at times we may get off the path of trust in God, his promises come to remind us of what is true. And whenever we allow the assurance of God's promises to encourage our faith, we move from defeating thoughts and attitudes of doubt and despair to the exhilarating freedom of purposeful living in God's kingdom.

Prayer: God of encouragement, as I look to your promises, may I experience the freedom that trust in them brings.

✷ ✷ ✷ ✷

FAITH IN ETERNITY'S BLESSINGS

God promised us an eternal home with him.

Verse for the Day: Jesus said, "Believe in God, believe also in me. In my Father's house there are many dwelling places. If it were not so, would I have told you that I go to prepare a place for you?" (John 14:1–2).

SEVERAL YEARS AGO, a New Zealand chief named Tamahana visited England and was taken to see a splendid mansion near London. As the chief was led through the estate, its spectacular opulence didn't seem to impress him. The host was intrigued by the chief's lack of awe, and so he showed him the beauty of the interior decor, such as the extravagant furniture that had been collected from every corner of the globe.

Chief Tamahana listened politely. Then the chief looked all around him and quietly replied, "Ah, my Father's house is finer than this."

Your father's house! thought the host, who knew Tamahana's father lived in a mud hut.

Tamahana repeated, "My Father's house is finer than this," and then he described his heavenly Father's mansions in his own unique and moving way—mansions Christ assured his followers were being prepared for them.

God's children know ultimate security—assurance of eternal life with their heavenly Father. No matter how grand or lowly the circumstances we find ourselves in today, Christ has promised us that there is a far better place we will one day inhabit. We can rejoice today as Chief Tamahana did in that English mansion, for all of the blessings of eternity are ours.

Prayer: I praise you, God, that my ultimate security lies in your promises of eternal blessings.

* * * *

PROMISES IN A PINCH
God's promises can reassure us in times of struggle.

Verse for the Day: "His divine power has given us everything needed for life and godliness, . . . Thus he has given us, through these things, his precious and very great promises" (2 Pet 1:3, 4).

NINETEENTH-CENTURY PREACHER Dwight L. Moody often called up Isaiah 50:7 in an emergency: "The Lord God helps me; therefore I have not been disgraced; therefore I have set my face like flint, and I know that I shall not be put to shame." Moody, great minister of the gospel, had a favorite promise of God to fall back on when life got tough.

Emily Lopez, who is 79 years old and a longtime believer in God's promises, has often turned to her favorite Scripture—Isaiah 41:10: "Do not fear, for I am with you, do not be afraid, for I am your God; I will strengthen you, I will help you, I will uphold you with my victorious right hand."

"When I was younger," Emily relates, "I was afraid of so many things, of things that were uncertain. I returned again and again to this verse to be reminded of God's strong presence in my life and to remember that he is in control."

The Bible is full of promises for those of us who will put their trust in God, bringing comfort and reassurance during life's more challenging moments and instilling courage in us for whatever lies ahead. Encourage your faith today by recalling a favorite promise from God's word or by searching out a new promise to hold on to.

Prayer: God, your promises comfort me because I know I can take you at your word.

* * * *

DRAWING COMFORT FROM FAITH

• • • •

A RETURN TO FAITH

**Returning to faith can bring
comfort to a restless soul.**

Verse for the Day: "Your face, Lord, do I seek" (Psa 27:8).

DOZENS OF BOOKS BEAR C. S. LEWIS'S name, among them *Mere Christianity, The Problem of Pain, The Great Divorce,* and *Surprised by Joy.* He is perhaps best known, however, for his popular children's series, *The Chronicles of Narnia.*

Clive Staples Lewis, nicknamed "Jack," was born in Belfast, Ireland, in 1898. When he was ten, his mother, Flora, died. Attempting to cope with his wife's death, Jack's father, Albert, placed his son in a boarding school, where his older brother, Warren, was already studying. The school's headmaster was an angry man, who took out his hostility on the boys at the school. In his search for some sense of comfort there, Jack began to pray and read his Bible.

After the school closed, Jack and his brother entered Malvern Cherbourg School in England and later Malvern College. Jack, however, not liking the conditions at this school either, asked his father to let him leave. Albert Lewis placed Jack under the private tutorage of W. T. Kirkpatrick, an atheist. Under his teacher's influence, Jack left behind his faith in God and turned his attention to philosophical and humanistic ideals.

Lewis received a scholarship to Oxford, and in 1917 he enlisted in the military. Nevertheless, he was allowed to remain at Oxford until he received his commission as a second lieutenant. While assigned to the front line, he was wounded and sent home where he was able to complete his studies. Though he graduated at the top of his class, there were no teaching positions open for him, so he studied for another year at Oxford. There he was impressed by a student named Nevill Coghill whose extraordinary intellect coupled with his Christian perspective contributed to a shift in Lewis's own views about the compatibility of faith and reason.

Lewis began reading the works of Christian authors and developed a close friendship with J.R.R. Tolkien, who wrote *The Lord of the Rings*. Lewis received an English fellowship at Magdalen College at Oxford in 1925, where his popularity as a lecturer rapidly grew. Students flocked to his classes, and Lewis had to seek a larger place in which to teach.

It was during this time that Lewis's search for truth increased, and he found that he had come almost full circle. From his boyhood faith, he had gone to not believing at all in a personal God to believing that an impersonal God-force existed in all things. His convictions then shifted to the existence of God, not as a force, but as a personal being.

Finally, in 1929, Lewis quit fighting what he had come to believe in his heart to be true. He prayed and expressed his trust in a personal God who is full of goodness and love. Returning to the assurances of his earlier faith, he found himself home again.

Prayer: God, when I return to the childlike faith I once knew, I realize again the comfort of your presence in my life.

$$* \quad * \quad * \quad *$$

COMFORTED BY GOD'S CARE
Faith comforts us as we are reminded that God cares for us.

Verse for the Day: "Cast all your anxiety on him, because he cares for you" (1 Pet 5:7).

*I*N A HOSPITAL, Doreen's minister was visiting her because she was about to undergo surgery. To offer comfort and encouragement, he spent time with her reading words of assurance from various passages of Scripture. Finally, before leaving, he prayed for God's protection, strength, and love to surround and guard Doreen as she faced the uncertainty of the surgery's outcome.

As the minister departed that day, he was unaware that there had been two patients in the hospital room who had drawn faith and comfort from his words. In another bed from behind a curtain that divided the room, Pearl had quietly listened to all that he had said. She, too, was facing surgery and a health problem with serious implications. Her anxious mind had been battling negative thoughts all day, but as she allowed the minister's words about God's love and care to permeate her heart and mind, her faith was renewed. A deep sense of peace filled her, and she was able to let go of her anxieties, replacing them with trust in God.

In our times of need, uncertainty, fear, and struggle, knowing that God is present and caring for us brings comfort and peace that nothing else can give. And as we experience the reality of God's presence in times of difficulty, our faith deepens and grows stronger, and our anxieties fall away.

Prayer: God of comfort, help me trust your care for me today and always.

* * * *

COMFORTED BY GRACE

As we trust God, he comforts us with his grace.

Verse for the Day: "His delight is not in the strength of the horse, nor his pleasure in the speed of a runner; but the Lord takes pleasure in those who fear him, in those who hope in his steadfast love" (Psa 147:10–11).

CHARLOTTE ELLIOTT'S BROTHER was a minister, who had a vision for establishing a special school for daughters of clergy. Excitement for the project grew as plans for a fundraising event were made. Charlotte, however, was in bad health and unable to help with her brother's endeavor. The night before the fundraiser, she could not sleep and started questioning her ability to be of service to God.

The following day while her friends attended the fundraiser, Charlotte stayed at home by herself. At first, thoughts about her weakness weighed her down, but then she compared her physical state with her spiritual state. She realized that just as God had forgiven her and accepted her simply by his grace and not by her own strength or her ability to do good works, so he loved and accepted her now in her weak physical state by holding her in his grace. Inspired by this insight, Charlotte Elliott wrote the stirring Christian hymn: "Just as I am."

Set to music, these words became the famous altar-call hymn of Billy Graham's worldwide gospel crusades. Though simple in its message, "Just as I Am" has had a powerful impact on the hearts of hundreds of thousands of people who have been moved by God's loving grace to receive his comforting forgiveness and assurance of eternal life.

Prayer: God of grace, I come to you for comfort in my weakness and trust that you will always hold me near.

′ ′ ′ ′

FAITH IN OTHERS

′ ′ ′ ′

KEEPING OUR FAITH IN OTHERS

Sometimes we have to be patient with someone to see the payoff.

Verse for the Day: "Get Mark and bring him with you, for he is useful in my ministry" (2 Tim 4:11).

RICHARD "RUBE" MARQUARD was a pitcher for the Indianapolis farm team. He was such a promising southpaw that the New York Giants paid him $11,000 in 1908—a considerable amount at that time! The press lauded Marquard as the next superstar.

In his first two seasons, however, Marquard tried so hard that he failed miserably. During those struggling seasons, he was dubbed the "eleven-thousand-dollar lemon." Then in 1911, "Rube" Marquard lived up to his advance billing, and in 1912, he won 19 consecutive games.

It's much easier to believe in someone after they've "hit their stride" than while they're at a low point. It takes a certain kind of faith to stick with someone else when the chips are down for them—especially when they've failed in some way.

Barnabas, the New Testament character who initially did a lot of traveling with the Apostle Paul, had that kind of faith in others. When Paul, as a new convert, had turned from killing Christians to being one, Barnabas stood up for him and spoke on his behalf when the Christian community was understandably skeptical. Yet because Barnabas was well respected, Paul was quickly received with open arms.

Later, Barnabas (his name means "son of encouragement") demonstrated his faith in a young apprentice named Mark. Apparently on an earlier journey with Paul and Barnabas, Mark had deserted them. Now, as they prepared for another journey, Barnabas was lobbying to bring Mark along. Paul did not want to risk another repeat abandonment, but Barnabas wanted to give Mark another chance. They had a falling out and parted company, Barnabas taking Mark and Paul departing on his journey with a man named Silas (see Acts 15:36-41).

Years later, as Paul wrote from his prison cell to another young minister, Timothy, he urged, "Get Mark and bring him with you, for he is useful in my ministry" (see "Verse for the Day"). It appears that Mark, at some point, had "hit his stride." And now Paul could see what Barnabas had believed was there all along.

Prayer: God, thank you that I can encourage others to succeed as I express faith in them.

* * * *

"I BELIEVE IN YOU!"

Expressing confidence in others can help them realize their dreams.

Verse for the Day: "Let each of you look . . . to the interests of others" (Phlp 2:4).

IN THE EARLY YEARS OF "SHOW BIZ," a young actor once jokingly made an interesting proposal to Sir Arthur Conan Doyle—the distinguished British physician and writer in whose play the young man was appearing. The actor, living on a slim weekly salary of ten dollars, suggested that he and Doyle make a lifetime agreement to split and share their salaries. Of course, the venerable Doyle, laughingly turned down the proposal, which he probably later wished he hadn't declined. For soon the young fellow became known to the world as Charlie Chaplin.

It's often much easier to believe in oneself than it is to have confidence in another. After all, we can control our own choices, and to an extent, our destiny. However, when it comes to others, we can only influence them, at best. Yet having vision for other people, believing in their potential, and backing them in their dreams can be not only risky but also highly rewarding.

Of course, there is a fine line between foolishness and faith. So while swapping salaries with minimum-wage workers is generally not advisable, expressing confidence in someone, backing them with our prayers, and reassuring them in the course of their quest could be the very thing that carries them through to success.

Prayer: As I back others with my faith in their potential, God, bless their efforts with success.

❦ ❦ ❦ ❦

A TURNING POINT

Demonstrating faith in others makes them feel valid and valued.

Verse for the Day: "*Anxiety weighs down the human heart, but a good word cheers it up*" (Prov 12:25).

*A*FTER INTRODUCING HIS STEAMBOAT as a new mode of transportation on American waterways, Robert Fulton reached an all-time low. The public mocked his invention, which deflated his sense of worth. One day, however, a man boarded Fulton's boat and asked Fulton how much it would cost to be taken to New York.

With no public interest in his vessel, Fulton hadn't even considered what he might charge passengers if he had any. He thought for a moment and then quoted a price of six dollars. When this stranger gave Fulton the money, he became the first paying steamboat passenger in history.

Years later, Fulton encountered the man once again and remarked, "The vivid emotions caused by your paying me that first passage money will always be remembered. That, sir, seemed the turning point in my destiny—the dividing line between light and darkness—the first actual recognition of my usefulness."

Robert Fulton experienced the power of having some-one put their faith in him when no one else would. It was the turning point in his destiny, he said, and it gave him a sense of usefulness. We have the power to en-courage others with expressions of confidence and trust in them. When we demonstrate faith in their ability or their character, they feel valid (relevant and meaningful), and they feel valued (worthwhile and esteemed). What a precious gift we can give to some-one who needs a boost of confidence today! For them, it may be just the thing they need to create a turning point in their life.

Prayer: God, as I express faith in others, let them know how much they are valued, not only by me, but also by you.

• • • •

ABLE TO TRUST OTHERS
When we have people in our lives whom we can trust, life is more enjoyable.

Verse for the Day: "What is desirable in a person is loyalty" (Prov 19:22).

IN AZERBAIJAN, THERE ONCE lived a peasant man named Shirili Muslimov, who claimed to be the oldest living person. He attributed his long life to hard work, a healthy diet, avoidance of harmful substances, and a general moderation in all things. He also mentioned his basic trust in others. Muslimov is said to have died at over 161 years old.

Contrast Muslimov's life with that of Joseph Stalin, who was extremely paranoid. In his fear of being the target of assassination plots, he alternated his sleeping quarters between eight bedrooms, which could be locked up like a safe. Certainly there were many differences between Muslimov and Stalin, given their different lives. Considering only the above accounts, however, there is a stark contrast between the two when it came to their ability to trust others. Interestingly, Muslimov identified the ability to trust as one of the factors that had carried him along for so many years.

A second contrast, perhaps stemming from their ability to trust people, was their enjoyment of life. Stalin, filled with paranoia, was disturbed and unhappy. Muslimov, on the other hand, was joyful and contented.

Surely it is not far-fetched to say that there is a correlation between having people in our lives we can trust and our sense of security and happiness in life. How blessed we are when we can trust others and be trusted by them in return.

Prayer: Thank you, God, for the trustworthy friends you have placed in my life.

* * * *

FREEDOM
FREEDOM IN GOD

* * * *

FREEDOM TO GROW
God provides all the right conditions
we need for spiritual growth.

*Verse for the Day: "Your faith is growing abun-
dantly, and the love for everyone of you for one
another is increasing"* (2 Thess 1:3).

A FEW MONTHS AGO, I took a cutting from one of
my mom's houseplants. I put it in water for
several weeks until it sprouted a number of roots. Then
I planted it in a little pot with some soil and added
plant food. Despite my best efforts, however, that poor
little plant is struggling to survive. Its leaves are curling
badly, and I sense that it is about to undergo a change
of color—from green to brown. It's obvious that I have
failed to supply the conditions that would free it to
grow and thrive. Put in plain terms: I am in no danger
of winning a green-thumb award anytime soon!

God, on the other hand, is the consummate gardener of
souls. He has both the concern for our welfare and the
intimate knowledge of our needs so we can grow freely.

He never gives our hearts too much shadow or too much sunlight (though at times we may beg for more). The soil, the air, the nourishment, the water—all of the circumstances for our particular disposition—are always just right. He makes no mistakes in his efforts to keep us strong and healthy.

We can be certain beyond a doubt that as we place ourselves daily in the care of expert hands, we will never stop experiencing the joy and freedom of spiritual growth that the Gardener's touch brings.

Prayer: My Creator, I trust you to give me everything I need to freely grow and thrive as one of your own.

* * * *

FREEDOM TO LOVE UNCONDITIONALLY
God's unconditional love frees us to love others unconditionally.

Verse for the Day: "Beloved, since God loved us so much, we also ought to love one another" (1 John 4:11).

WILLIAM BOOTH FOUNDED the Salvation Army, but many believe his wife, Catherine, was the driving force behind their compassionate endeavor to help and minister to the poor and needy in England.

A story from Catherine's childhood is told that illustrates her heart of sympathy. One day, as she was playing by a public road, Catherine saw a constable hauling a prisoner to jail. A swarm of people followed them, jeering at the convict. As Catherine watched this procession, her compassion was stirred for this prisoner. Because he appeared friendless, she made herself his friend by hurrying to his side and accompanying him down the street. She wanted him to know that someone cared about him whether he was guilty or not.

The compassion of that young girl reminds us that while we were still unlovely, lonely sinners, Christ died to forgive us and extend God's compassion to us. It is this agape love or "unconditional God-love" that inspires the kind of love in us that reaches out to those who would otherwise be difficult, if not impossible, to care for.

While unconditional love does not mean that we are blind to the wrongs others may have committed, it does mean that we can reach past their unsavory baggage to touch them with a love they may never have experienced before: love without condition—God's love.

Prayer: God, your love for me compels me to love others who need to know how much you love them.

*   *   *   *

ATTRACTIVE FREEDOM

As we live in the freedom of God's truth, others will be attracted to us.

Verse for the Day: "You will know the truth, and the truth will make you free" (John 8:32).

*A*S WE MATURE and grow more wise, we realize that God has given us not only the truth of his word but also the understanding of years to illuminate that truth, making it more plain and evident to us. As the truth has become incorporated into our lives, we have become increasingly enlightened by it, gaining freedom from youth's naiveté, immaturity, insecurity, and pride.

When Dale decided to return to work after several years of retirement, he was uncertain how his presence would affect his younger male coworkers. Dale is confident and kind, free from the need to posture or compete with his coworkers. His freedom is like a magnet, drawing a crowd of young men during lunch breaks. In the small lunch room, they like to ask Dale's input regarding issues they're facing. They like to be around him and find out what makes him "tick." They want what he has.

Without being overbearing, Dale talks about insights he has gained and the truth he has discovered through life experience and Scripture. Dale realizes these men see in him a freedom they long for, including freedom from worry, fear, uncertainty, and purposelessness.

"There is no substitute for the freedom that comes from getting a hold of what's true in this life," Dale says. "When people see such freedom in action, they realize that's what they've been looking for all along."

Our lives are living advertisements to the world when they're permeated by truth and characterized by the freedom truth brings. Such lives draw others to the truth God offers and impart the gift of freedom.

Prayer: God, thank you that I can live as one who has been freed by your truth so that I can lead others to freedom.

* * * *

SET FREE FROM GUILT
God's love sets us free from guilt.

Verse for the Day: "If the Son makes you free, you will be free indeed" (John 8:36).

AS ONE OF PRESIDENT NIXON'S primary aides, Chuck Colson was known as the President's toughest hatchet man. In 1974, however, Colson pleaded guilty to a Watergate-related charge and was given a one-to-three-year prison sentence.

Before his sentencing, Colson had visited a friend whose life had been so changed by a newfound faith in God that Colson wanted to know what had changed him. The friend talked about God's transforming power and the forgiveness he had in Christ's love.

Colson, desperate for such peace and forgiveness, asked God to help him take control of his life. Not long after, he attended a prayer conference and was mocked by the news media for having "gotten religion." For Colson, however, ridicule could not alter the reality of what he had experienced. With a sense of freedom from the guilt of his moral failures, yet knowing he would have to pay the consequences for them, he entered the prosecutor's office and cleared up the record as to what he had done in the Watergate crimes.

While in prison, Colson learned that his son had been caught with marijuana and that his father had died, leaving his mother alone. Adding to his frustration was the knowledge that the other Watergate offenders— sentenced by a different judge—had been released from prison. Colson became increasingly discouraged.

Then, a congressperson who was a part of Colson's prayer support group made an unbelievable exchange. He went through the appropriate channels to arrange to serve the rest of Colson's sentence so that he could be home with his family. God's love had freed Colson from his guilty conscience, and now, exhibited through a friend, it would free him from prison.

When Colson was interviewed at the twentieth anniversary of Watergate, Mike Wallace asked him how he looked back on his Watergate experience. Colson told Wallace that he thanked God for it because he had learned the greatest lesson of his life—that of being freed by God's love and forgiveness.

Prayer: God, thank you for your love and forgiveness, which completely free me from guilt.

❧ ❧ ❧ ❧

FREEDOM IN FORGIVENESS

❧ ❧ ❧ ❧

FREE TO FORGIVE OTHERS
When we have experienced forgiveness, we are free to forgive others.

Verse for the Day: "Be kind to one another, tenderhearted, forgiving one another, as God in Christ has forgiven you" (Eph 4:32).

As THE EVENTS OF WORLD WAR II unfolded, Corrie Ten Boom, a Dutch woman, lived and worked with her father and sister in her father's watch-repair shop in the Netherlands. During the German occupation, the Ten Booms took in a number of Jews, protecting them from the Nazis. To keep their guests from being discovered in the event of a surprise search of their home, they arranged to have a secret room built.

As anticipated, late one night the Nazis came to ransack the residence. Much to the consternation of members of the search party, however, neither the room nor its inhabitants was ever discovered. Despite the Nazis' inability to uncover the Jews' whereabouts, the Ten Boom family was taken away and imprisoned.

In her book *The Hiding Place,* Corrie described her experiences as a prisoner in a Nazi concentration camp. She and her sister endured extreme hardship and cruelty at the hands of the guards there. Though her sister didn't survive the ordeal, Corrie was mistakenly released due to a clerical error.

With her life forever changed by what she had been through, Corrie began writing and speaking about what it had been like in the prison camp and how she believed God had helped her endure.

In 1947, Corrie spoke to parishioners in Munich about God's love and forgiveness. Afterward, a man approached her and thanked her for showing him that even he could be forgiven. She recognized the tall, aged man as one of the exceptionally cruel guards who had mistreated her sister and her in the camp. He explained to Corrie that he had become a follower of Christ, and extending his hand to her, he asked for her forgiveness.

With conflicting emotions swirling within her, Corrie struggled to know how to respond. In a moment of clarity, she knew that just as God's forgiveness had been freely given to her, she needed to freely extend forgiveness to this penitent man. In desperation, she silently prayed, "Jesus, help me!" and thrust her hand into the hand of her former tormentor. Upon doing so, she was freed from her anger and resentment as it melted into genuine forgiveness, inspired by God's love.

Prayer: God, forgiveness is not easy, but thank you that as I forgive, I will experience new levels of freedom.

* * * *

FORGIVING OURSELVES
To fully experience the freedom of forgiveness, we must forgive ourselves.

Verse for the Day: "There is therefore now no condemnation for those who are in Christ Jesus" (Rom 8:1).

WHEN MEMBERS OF THE religious elite wanted to see how Jesus' teaching on forgiveness could reconcile with their religious laws, they brought a woman who had been caught in adultery—a sin that required the death penalty by stoning according to the Mosaic Law.

After stooping down to write something in the sand, Jesus calmly looked up at the faces so full of self-righteous indignation and said, "Whoever is without sin, let him cast the first stone."

One by one, the crowd dispersed. When they were all gone, Jesus asked the guilty woman, "Where are your accusers?"

"There aren't any," she replied.

"Neither do I condemn you," Jesus said. "Go and leave your life of sin."

Forgiven by God. Forgiven, in a sense, by others. Now there was only one obstacle left for complete freedom for this woman. Would she accept the forgiveness extended to her and so forgive herself? Or would she pick up stones of self-loathing and shame and throw them again and again at herself as a form of punishment for failure?

No more is said about this woman's life in the Scriptures, but we do know very well about our own experiences with failure and sin. Whether we've been found out by others or not, we are familiar with feelings, such as remorse and regret, that accompany our failure. Of course, these feelings are good when they serve their purpose, driving us to seek forgiveness. Yet when we carry them for years on end—long after God has announced our freedom—they become destructive stones with which we beat up our souls unnecessarily.

I like to think that woman, brought before Jesus that day, was so overwhelmed with Jesus' demonstration of love and forgiveness toward her that she experienced a freedom that transformed her life. I like to believe that she no longer focused on her failure but on her newfound identity as one who was set free from the past to live in a bright future of renewed hope. For that is exactly what the Lord offered her. And it is what he offers each of us every time we seek his forgiveness.

If we're still casting stones at ourselves today, it's time to put them down, and by receiving God's forgiveness, forgive ourselves as well.

Prayer: God, you have not condemned me but you have completely forgiven me; please help me now to forgive myself.

*   *   *   *

FREEDOM IN GOD'S FORGIVENESS

God's forgiveness frees us to enjoy a fresh start.

Verse for the Day: "The Holy Spirit also testifies to us, . . . 'I will remember their sins and their lawless deeds no more'" (Heb 10:15, 17).

IT IS REPORTED THAT when Moravian missionaries first went to the Eskimos, there was no apparent word in their native language for forgiveness. To relate the gospel of Christ's forgiveness, the missionaries needed to find a word that would aptly convey what it means to forgive. So they strung together a number of words to form the compound *issumagijoujungnainermik*—a long word, which simply means "not being able to think about it anymore."

That freshly coined word in the Eskimo language conveys exactly the nature of God's forgiveness for his children. Those who trust in his pardon receive complete freedom from their sins, for God essentially forgets the past. In place of their past failure to live up to God's standard, God gives each of his children the clean moral record of Christ himself. It's an extraordinary exchange offered by the living God to anyone—without exception—who will receive it.

Although we ourselves may still recall the past at times, the Bible assures us that God loves and forgives us. Thus, when we receive God's forgiveness, where our sin is concerned, he is "not able to think about it anymore."

Prayer: God, your forgiveness frees me to live as one who is lighthearted and happy to be alive.

* * * *

FREEDOM TO BE FORGIVEN
Accepting forgiveness brings freedom to myself and to others.

Verse for the Day: "Happy are those whose transgression is forgiven" (Psa 32:1).

*A*H, MISTAKES! Whether we feel we have the freedom to make them or not, we will certainly make plenty of them. In the process of learning, growing, and interacting with others, make no mistake, mistakes will abound.

Fern was serving grape juice to her grandson Eric when she lost her grip on the bottle and some of the liquid spilled on the boy's pants, staining them. "Oh, I'm so sorry!" she exclaimed to Eric and then to her daughter-in-law. Tears filled her eyes. She knew she had ruined the trousers.

"That's OK, Mom," Shirley reassured. "They were getting too small for him anyway, and we were about to go shopping for a new pair."

"I'll pay for them!" Fern cried.

"No, Mom. There's no need for that, really. Please don't worry," Shirley pleaded. "It was just an accident."

However, Fern couldn't relax until she had replaced the pants with a new pair.

Clearly, it is not the freedom to make mistakes that is in short supply in our human experience. Rather, it is the freedom to receive forgiveness for our mistakes. Perhaps it's good to remind ourselves every now and then that by allowing ourselves to be forgiven by others, we free them to accept our forgiveness in return. Receiving a pardon with joy lets us experience the wonderful freedom that forgiveness brings to our relationships.

Prayer: God, you are the ultimate pardon-giver; help me receive forgiveness from others as from you.

* * * *

FULFILLMENT
FULFILLMENT IN RELATIONSHIPS

. . . .

A GRANDPARENT'S LOVE FOR A CHILD

Having the love and trust of young children fulfills our souls in a special way.

Verse for the Day: "May you see your children's children" (Psa 128:6).

IN THE PAINTING "A HELPING HAND," the French artist Emile Ranouf portrays an elderly man and a little girl seated in a boat. Evidently he is her grandfather.

While both their hands are grasping a heavy oar, he gazes at her with grandfatherly affection. It appears that he has asked her to help him row the boat, and in her earnest attempt to be of assistance, her face reflects her belief that she is doing much of the work. Yet it's clear that he is powering the boat through the waters.

The wordless image of that grandfather with the little girl captures the essence of what each grandparent feels when they are entrusted with the precious love of a child. At times the experience is so wonderful that it can feel almost like an ache!

Thankfully God has given us the privilege of experiencing the fulfillment of such a relationship when we nurture and encourage our grandchildren in their earliest stages of life. For there is no one quite like a grandparent able to lay a hand on the oar and be the silent strength to help them cut through the waters of life. Certainly this is a reflection of God's love for us.

Prayer: God, how you must love me, for I know how deeply I love the children you have entrusted to my care.

* * * *

FULFILLMENT IN GOD'S LOVE
We find what we've been missing when we let God into our lives.

~⟨♡⟩~

Verse for the Day: "As the Father has loved me, so I have loved you; abide in my love.... I have said these things to you so that my joy may be in you, and that your joy may be complete" (John 15:9, 11).

MITTENS THE CAT came to live with me on the last day of 1998. Her owners were moving to Europe, and she needed a new home. Being a sucker for a feline face, I was more than willing to adopt her. She's a beauty: a longhair, mostly Siamese, petite, and blue-eyed. I'd hold her in a heartbeat, pet her, and pamper her... if only she'd let me. But Mittens is still grieving the loss of her home and family, and she will have none of my comforting. So I wait.

I wait for the day when she'll realize she has my undivided love and attention, the day she'll discover she can meow and I'll ask "how high?" Right now she has no idea the perks and privileges she'll have when she finally finds it in her heart to give me a chance. But until then...

This little exercise in waiting for Mittens to come around has put me in mind of how my relationship with God has developed over time. In the transfer of my trust from parents and other people to Providence, I haven't always been easy to convince that God's love is trustworthy. I wonder what it has been like for God, who knows all of the benefits and blessings he wants to give me, but who waits with infinite patience for me to welcome them.

I now know from experience that making God wait for me is my loss, not his. For every time I reach a new level of trust in our relationship, I realize what I've been missing and wonder why I waited so long to let love in.

Yet relationships are a process, and coming to understand the love God has for me is part of the process of growing closer to him. I can only say that I'm glad beyond explaining that the process is well underway. It's the best kind of relationship—the kind a person looks and looks for, but can find nowhere else.

Prayer: God, your love for me is unsurpassed, and in it I find what I've been looking for.

* * * *

THE BLESSING OF TIME

Our relationships become more fulfilling as they are framed in the space of extra time.

～◎～

Verse for the Day: "For everything there is a season, and a time for every matter under heaven" (Eccl 3:1).

OFTEN IN OUR LATER YEARS, the frantic pace of life lets up: The children are raised; the mortgage is paid; and we've learned that it's wisest to take on only a few things at a time and to do them well. Our life begins to have space and time in which we can step back and relish the events, activities, and relationships in our lives. Visits with family take on new specialness. Get-togethers with friends can be leisurely instead of hurried. The children we love—especially grandchildren—are the apples of our eye as we watch them grow. With this acquired "breathing room" of reclaimed time, our significant relationships take on a new beauty, and from them we gain a deeper sense of fulfillment.

In her book *Gift from the Sea,* Anne Morrow Lindbergh observed, "For it is only framed in space that beauty blooms. Only in space are events and objects and people unique and significant—and therefore beautiful. A tree has significance if one sees it against the empty face of the sky. A note in music gains significance from the silences on either side. A candle flowers in the space of night. Even small and casual things take on significance if they are washed in space, like a few autumn grasses in one corner of an Oriental painting, the rest of the page bare."

Of course, all things have significance whether they are framed by space or not. Yet it is in our ability to perceive them as significant that they are given an area all their own. And so, if we are fortunate enough to find that our schedule is not as full as it once was, we discover that the space of time we now have is a blessing—a frame for moments with those we love.

Prayer: God, thank you for the time you provide for me to savor the loving relationships in my life.

❧ ❧ ❧ ❧

TREATED WITH DIGNITY

We experience a sense of fulfillment when others treat us with dignity.

Verse for the Day: Jesus said to her, "Daughter, your faith has made you well; go in peace, and be healed of your disease" (Mark 5:34).

THERE'S A WELL-KNOWN STORY about the great Russian writer, Leo Tolstoy, which provides interesting insight into his character. Evidently he encountered a beggar on a street one day, who implored him for some coins.

Tolstoy reached into his pockets, but finding them empty, he sadly said, "Please don't be angry with me, my brother, but I have nothing with me. If I did I would gladly give it to you."

The beggar's face beamed as he replied, "You have given me more than I asked for. You have called me 'brother.'"

There is nothing quite like being treated with respect and dignity by others to make us feel valued. On the other hand, when we are treated with contempt or indifference, our sense of worth can plummet, making us feel unworthy.

In Jesus' day, women were often treated as mere property, as objects rather than valued persons. In the passage from which the "Verse for the Day" was drawn, the woman whom Jesus healed at first was afraid to make herself known to him. After all, she was just a woman. Moreover, she was a woman with an incurable illness. Her condition had persisted for 12 years, and the nature of her illness had made her an outcast in her society. In fact, if she were married, even her husband would not be permitted to touch her under Levitical law, because her bleeding made her unclean.

Yet Jesus urged her to come forward, calling her "daughter"—a term of love and acceptance. He announced for all to hear that she had been healed, and then he sent her on her way in peace. After 12 years of utter rejection, this woman experienced the fulfillment of love, respect, and dignity. She was human again.

This is God's attitude toward all of us. We are of infinite value to him. In a crowd, he would not be ashamed to speak with us, to treat us with loving respect, and to call us his own. This is the ultimate pronouncement of our human dignity and worth, and we are lifted up inside when others acknowledge and affirm it as well.

Prayer: God, you determine my value, but I also thank you for those who treat me with the dignity my soul craves.

* * * *

THE FULFILLMENT OF UNITY

The fulfillment we experience in unity is possible when we focus on our similarities.

Verse for the Day: "How very good and pleasant it is when kindred live together in unity!" (Psa 133:1).

IN 1730 GEORGE WHITEFIELD, a 26-year-old evangelist, arrived in the United States. American believers from various denominations embraced him as a fellow worker in Christ. These Christians included Baptists, Presbyterians, Quakers, Lutherans, Congregationalists, Dutch Reformed, and all who proclaimed the truth of the gospel.

On his way to North America, Whitefield wrote to a friend, "The partition wall [of prejudice] has for some time been broken down out of my heart, and I can truly say whoever loves the Lord Jesus, 'the same is my brother, and sister, and mother.'"

Whitefield had learned the secret of unity among believers. He knew that when people share common ground on essential issues, they must remain focused and work together on these grounds. Whitefield realized, too, that where nonessentials are concerned, freedom is the rule and respect is the proper attitude.

As we work to establish and maintain our relationships with others, we will find the pleasant fulfillment of unity as we look for and stand together on our common ground. Meanwhile, we can allow our love for one another to bridge the gap between our differences.

Prayer: God, grant that I may live in unity with those whom you have placed in my life.

∎ ∎ ∎ ∎

FULFILLMENT IN ACCOMPLISHMENTS

∎ ∎ ∎ ∎

THE ROAD TO FULFILLMENT
We can find fulfillment in our honest attempts to achieve our goals.

∼◯∼

Verse for the Day: "I have fought the good fight, I have finished the race, I have kept the faith" (2 Tim 4:7).

IN HIS 1910 SPEECH IN Sorbonne, France, Theodore Roosevelt said, "It is not the critic who counts.... The credit belongs to the man who is actually in the arena; whose face is marred by dust and sweat and blood; ... who at the best knows in the end the triumph of high achievement; and who at the worst, if he fails, at least fails while daring greatly, so that his place shall never be with those cold and timid souls who know neither victory nor defeat."

R. G. LeTourneau was such a man. Of course, LeTourneau's successes are relatively well known. Many can still recall that on June 6, 1944, accompanying the D-Day invasion at Normandy was a remarkable array of machinery. LeTourneau had designed and manufactured a good deal of the equipment used in that effort. Perhaps still more people are aware that in civilian endeavors, LeTourneau's company built some of the world's most colossal machinery, including earth movers, portable offshore drilling rigs, and missile launchers.

What many do not know about LeTourneau's success is that struggle, failure, and loss had preceded it. In his early teens, LeTourneau dropped out of school and found a job at a factory in Portland, Oregon. There he worked shoveling sand and dirt, and by age 16, he had grown into a brawny young man full of inventive ideas.

When LeTourneau moved to California, he had worked more than 30 jobs to make ends meet. At age 28, he married a girl 12 years younger than he, and sadly their first child died in infancy. Difficulties mounted for the young couple as LeTourneau broke his neck in a stock-car crash. Then at 31, LeTourneau found himself deep in debt due to the bad decisions of a business partner.

Rather than attempt to escape responsibility for the debt, LeTourneau dissolved the partnership and sought a loan from a banker, promising he would repay every cent. When the banker asked how he intended to make payment, LeTourneau simply held up his strong hands. The banker extended the loan, giving LeTourneau the capital he needed to buy the equipment and go into the earth-moving business.

LeTourneau paid back his loan and, of course, became an extraordinary businessperson. Not only was he able to enjoy the fulfillment of accomplishments brought about by his determination and hard work, but he also found fulfillment in sharing his financial surplus with many people, institutions, and causes.

Prayer: I have found fulfillment, God, in hard-won successes as you have seen me through my many struggles.

* * * *

I Finally Did It!
Persevering to accomplish a goal brings great fulfillment.

Verse for the Day: "We will reap at harvest time, if we do not give up" (Gal 6:9).

AFTER RETIREMENT, Ben decided he would begin work on patenting some equipment designs and marketing them. It would be relatively simple, he thought. Once he had immersed himself in the process, however, it became increasingly complicated. A patent attorney had to write the documents for the patenting offices. He had to electronically draft his drawings. Ben's simple ideas were creating a paper trail much longer than the road to success he had first imagined. Setbacks often slowed progress, and Ben often wondered why he had ever wanted to try such an endeavor.

During this process, Ben acquired a partner, Art, who was a long-time friend and who saw the potential in Ben's ideas. Art's belief in the project gave Ben the push he needed to persevere even when it seemed the finish line would never come into view.

The payoff finally came not long ago when, patents in hand, Ben was able to present his ideas and prototype to potential buyers. Sold on his inventions, they eagerly snapped up the opportunity to outfit their machines with his equipment.

Ben hasn't forgotten the sweat and tears that went into his accomplishment, and if you asked him whether he would do it all over again, he'd hesitate before saying yes. But the truth is the fulfillment he's experienced from reaching the goal line makes him stand a little taller.

Prayer: God, when I think of my own accomplishments, I enjoy a sense of fulfillment that no one can take away.

* * * *

FULFILLMENT IN WORK AND ACTIVITIES

. . . .

FULFILLMENT IN EXCELLENCE

**When we are committed to excellence,
we find fulfillment in all that we do.**

*Verse for the Day: "Do your best to present yourself
to God as one approved by him, a worker
who has no need to be ashamed"* (2 Tim 2:15).

OVER TWO AND A HALF CENTURIES AGO, Antonio Stradivari lived and worked as a violin maker in Italy. Once he had established his own workshop, he maintained the standard that no violin should ever leave his shop until it was as near perfection as humanly possible. "God needs violins to send his music into the world," he said, "and if my violins are defective, God's music will be spoiled."

As he toiled at his workbench in Cremona, Stradivari vowed, "Other men will make other violins, but no man shall make a better one." And though he died in 1737, the quality of his workmanship to this day remains unparalleled.

Whether we're making violins, building birdhouses, or baking pies, our work bears evidence of our commitment to excellence. Although Stradivari conceded that perfection was not possible, his desire to come as near to it as possible is commendable.

Of course, reaching toward perfection for perfection's sake is mere nit-picking and will drive us and those around us crazy. But striving for excellence to bring honor to the name of God and to be the kind of "worker who has no need to be ashamed" is deeply fulfilling.

Prayer: As I strive for excellence in all that I do, God, may people see a reflection of your excellence in me.

* * * *

THE BAZAAR QUEENS
Striving for excellence in our activities gives a sense of pride and fulfillment.

Verse for the Day: "Whatever your hand finds to do, do with your might" (Eccl 9:10).

ESTHER AND DORA ARE the queens of organizing their church's annual craft bazaar. They masterminded the first event, and they're still going strong.

Each year, people comment on how well planned and enjoyable the bazaar is from the variety of the crafters who participate to the well-stocked and reasonably priced snack bar. Because word has spread around the community about the quality of their craft fair, lots of people want to participate. Veterans of the event always reserve their spaces early, a lesson latecomers learn quickly. Esther and Dora must always regretfully turn down last-minute booth applications.

On the big day, as Dora and Esther accommodate the needs of the crafters, oversee the snack bar workers, and troubleshoot when necessary, their energies drain past empty. It's not surprising then, that when all the crafters have gone home and there is only the drone of vacuum cleaners and chatter of the clean-up crew, the two women confide in one another:

"What a lot of work! Do you think you want to do it again next year?" Esther asks.

"Well, with the way I feel now," Dora says, "definitely not!"

Then exchanging weary but wry smiles, they know they will be back next year.

Prayer: God, thank you for the activities in my life that give me satisfaction and for the energy to do them.

❧ ❧ ❧ ❧

THE FULFILLMENT OF GIVING

The activity of benevolence completes
and fulfills us as human beings.

*Verse for the Day: "Those who are generous are blessed, for
they share their bread with the poor"* (Prov 22:9).

GEORGE PEABODY, A RICH MERCHANT of the nineteenth century, was exceedingly liberal in giving
his money to humanitarian causes. One of his favorite
philanthropic projects was the construction of tenement houses in London. At a social gathering in Baltimore, someone asked him which he enjoyed more—
making money or giving it away.

"I think it is a great pleasure to make money," he
replied. "And when the idea was first suggested to me
that I give money away, it did not please me at all. In
fact, it distressed me. But I thought the matter over and
concluded that I would try it on a small scale. So I built
the first of the model tenement houses in London. It
was a hard pull. But after it was done, I went around
among the poor people living in the rooms so clean
and comfortable, and I had quite a new feeling. I enjoyed it very much. So I gave some more and the feeling increased. And now I can truly say that, much as

I enjoyed making my money, I enjoyed giving it away a great deal better."

What is that deep feeling of satisfaction we get whenever we extend a gift—the fruit of our labors—to another less fortunate person? It is fulfillment—a sense of being completed in some way. For we were created in the image of our Creator, who is benevolent toward all of humanity, and whenever we imitate his benevolence, we are, in a sense, fulfilling part of the purpose for which we were created.

Prayer: God, thank you for the opportunities you give me to experience the fulfillment of being benevolent to others, just as you are benevolent toward me.

* * * *

GRATITUDE
GRATEFUL FOR SIMPLE GIFTS

. . . .

THE GIFT OF TODAY

Being grateful for the present makes us
able to fully experience life's best moments.

*Verse for the Day: "Go, eat your bread with enjoyment,
and drink your wine with a merry heart; for God has
long ago approved what you do"* (Eccl 9:7).

AMERICAN CLERIC HENRY WARD BEECHER once said,
"No matter what looms ahead, if you can eat
today, enjoy the sunlight today, mix good cheer with
friends today, enjoy it and bless God for it. Do not look
back on happiness—or dream of it in the future. You
are only sure of today; do not let yourself be cheated
out of it."

Regretting the past and dreading the future: There are
no two more sure ways to destroy today's blessings.
Think of the people you know who never seem to stop
lamenting what happened years ago or perhaps even
yesterday. Living with a constant sense of failure or
worthlessness, they are incapable of enjoying today's

fresh start. Sadly, they may even feel they don't deserve to enjoy a fresh start.

In contrast, yet as tragic, are those individuals who allow their concern about what might happen tomorrow to eclipse today's sunlight. What-ifs and somedays are their consuming concerns.

"You are only sure of today," Henry Ward Beecher reminds us.

We have only today. Yesterday is not reclaimable; tomorrow is not ours to presume upon. But today, right now, is our gift of the precious thing we cling to so tenaciously: life. The present moment is life we can look at—stare into its face. The past and future are not really life; life is only ever right here with us as we live moment by moment.

We are blessed today if we can catch a glimpse of God's creation and his gifts in whatever form they may take. If we can stop to stroke a puppy, view a garden, enjoy a favorite flavor, hear a friendly voice, smell a warm meal, or enjoy life in any sense today, we have succeeded in living in the present and receiving its gift.

Prayer: Thank you for today, God, and for its many gifts that meet me at every turn.

❧ ❧ ❧ ❧

SIMPLE GIFTS OF KINDNESS
Simple gifts of kindness from others can deeply arouse our gratitude.

Verse for the Day: "It was kind of you to share my distress. . . . no church shared with me in the matter of giving and receiving, except you alone" (Phlp 4:14–15).

AFTER PRESIDENT LINCOLN RECEIVED an elderly woman into his office, he inquired, "What can I do for you, Madam?"

"Mr. President, I have come here today not to ask any favor for myself or for anyone. I heard that you were very fond of cookies, and I came here to bring you this basket of cookies!"

While the woman gave the cookies to the president, tears dropped from his eyes. At first he could not speak; he was so moved. Finally, he said to her, "My good woman, your thoughtful and unselfish deed greatly moves me. Thousands have come into this office since I became president, but you are the first one to come asking no favor for yourself or somebody else!"

Recalling simple gifts of kindness we have received from family, friends, and even complete strangers can arouse our sense of gratitude and remind us that we are loved.

I recall an act of kindness during my childhood. This cherished memory still stirs my gratitude toward a neighbor, who baked a cake for my fifth birthday and gave me a tablet filled with rainbow-colored sheets of paper. Though our families were not in the habit of recognizing one another's birthdays, this dear woman had gone out of her way to make me feel special.

Today, let your thoughts be filled with memories of simple gifts of kindness you have received. Let your gratitude be brought to a new level as you realize again how much others care for you.

Prayer: God, thank you for the way you show your care for me through the gifts of kindness I receive from others.

THE SIMPLE GIFT OF HUGGING
Hugs give the gift of human touch.

Verse for the Day: "And [Jesus] took [the children] up in his arms, laid his hands on them, and blessed them" (Mark 10:16).

"THANKS, I NEEDED THAT," said Phyllis as her granddaughter embraced her warmly. They held on for a minute just to enjoy the moment of togetherness.

A myriad of studies have been conducted to research the effects and power of human touch. Conclusive evidence has been gathered, proving that touch is vital to our well-being. When you give and receive hugs, you experience the effects of a veritable wonder drug, and this is one drug that has no undesirable effects, no expensive prescription to fill, and no time limit.

So many benefits from such a simple gift! And it just makes sense that the best way to express gratitude for such a gift would be to exercise it freely. So what are we waiting for? Let's hug away!

Prayer: Thank you, dear God, for the gift of human touch I can give and receive through hugs today.

* * * *

THE SIMPLE GIFT OF MUSIC
Music is a special gift
that touches our emotions.

Verse for the Day: "David took the lyre and played it with his hand, and Saul would be relieved and feel better" (1 Sam 16:23).

WHEN I WAS A YOUNG GIRL, I took piano lessons. I tended to enjoy playing songs that were very melodic or in some way beautifully haunting, and I memorized several such pieces. In the evenings,

I would play them for my father, who would lean back in his easy chair, close his eyes, and absorb the sound. Sometimes as he relaxed, he would even doze off.

The range of moods and feelings we experience as humans can be expressed in music as in no other medium. Music can move us to tears. It can urge us to dance. Hymns and praise choruses turn our hearts toward worship. Anthems call to our sense of national pride and loyalty. Classical and easy-listening music calm our nerves. Even tunes we remember from years ago can reach into the past and bring back old memories and feelings. Such is the strange and wonderful power of music.

Our Creator has given us music as a gift for our enjoyment and as a means of expressing our thoughts and emotions. Is there a special song or kind of music you love to dance to? Is there a hymn that has been particularly meaningful to your faith? What song has been running through your mind lately, putting a spring in your step and a smile on your face? God delights in our enjoyment of his gifts. Don't hesitate to thank him for his gift of music today. In fact, you might even choose to express your thoughts to him in a song of praise.

Prayer: Music is a wonderful gift you've given me, God; it can stir and lift my spirit as nothing else can.

GRATEFUL FOR OPPORTUNITIES

* * * *

THE OPPORTUNITY TO LIVE FULLY

**Gratitude for being alive energizes
our efforts to live complete lives.**

*Verse for the Day: "Even those who live
many years should rejoice in them all"* (Eccl 11:8).

*E*ACH YEAR OF OUR LIVES is an opportunity to create,
learn, discover, and accomplish still more than we
ever have before. Those who seize the glory of each day
demonstrate deep gratefulness for the gift of life. Such
inspiring individuals become more, not less, as their
age increases. Consider the following well-known
people:

Moses was 80 when God called him to lead his people,
and indeed he did lead the Hebrews out of Egyptian
bondage. In her seventies, Harriet Tubman worked
with black women's organizations and was a delegate to
the first convention of the National Federation of Afro-
American women in 1896.

Michelangelo painted the ceiling of the Sistine Chapel
when he was almost 90. When she was 71, Katharine

Hepburn won her unprecedented fourth Academy Award for acting for her performance in *On Golden Pond*. In his eighties, Richard Strauss composed some of his best music.

Eleanor Roosevelt wrote her autobiography in 1961 at age 77. In 1962 she sponsored civil rights hearings in Washington as part of her ongoing activism in the civil rights movement. Benjamin Franklin studied philosophy after he was 50, became the ambassador to France at 78, and produced his autobiography in his eighties.

Jane Addams, human rights activist, working for better housing for the poor was traveling and giving speeches worldwide at age 65, often working 14 to 18 hours a day. Victor Hugo wrote *Les Miserables* at 62. In her fifties, Annie Oakley was acting, riding, and shooting in a traveling Western show.

We probably won't enjoy the fame these individuals had, but such fame does not make one's life more or less significant or successful in the Creator's esteem. Certainly he smiles whenever he sees one of his older children taking hold of his gift called life, tearing open the wrapping, trying it on for size, and dancing joyfully as its beautiful colors fill their days.

Prayer: God, let all that I do today become a shout of praise and thanksgiving to you for this gift of life.

❧ ❧ ❧ ❧

Thanks for Opportunity-Makers

We can thank God for the people in our lives who have created good opportunities for us.

Verse for the Day: "Let us give thanks" (Heb 12:28).

WHEN YOU THINK of some of the great opportunities others have provided for you in life, what names and faces come to your mind? A parent? A teacher? An employer? A friend?

One of the opportunity-makers I was fortunate to know in college was Dr. Ralph Woodworth. I was one of his journalism students as he was nearing retirement. Thankfully, he never saw approaching retirement as an excuse to stop helping his students succeed.

My first job out of college came to me largely because Dr. Woodworth created an opportunity for me to network with prospective employers. During finals week of my senior year, he drove a vanload of students to a publishers' convention (several states away) and made sure we had our resumes in hand. Looking back, I can see that it was a big sacrifice for him, an act of selflessness that gave me the chance I needed to begin doing the work I love most.

What good jobs have you landed, interesting places have you visited, exciting experiences have you had, or wonderful people have you met due to someone else's opportunity-making on your behalf?

We can thank God for these special people he has placed in our lives, for through them he has given us gifts of opportunity that remain with us as reminders of his love and care.

Prayer: God, thank you for the opportunity-makers you've placed in my life, who demonstrate your love for me.

* * * *

GRATEFUL FOR FREEDOM'S OPPORTUNITIES

We can be grateful for the opportunities afforded us by our freedom.

Verse for the Day: "Be careful then how you live . . . making the most of the time . . . giving thanks to God the Father at all times . . ." (Eph 5:15, 16, 20).

MANY YEARS AGO, *The New York Times* told the story of a Polish immigrant. She and her husband had come to America six years earlier with only $2.60 and few possessions. Nevertheless, she had great hope for her future.

"There is something in the air of America," she said, "that filled my soul with a feeling of freedom and independence. This begot strength. There is no one here to lead you by the hand and order you about. We believed in the future and the future did not disappoint us."

Her husband eventually secured a respected position in society. Their dreams for a happy new life came true as they moved into a comfortable home.

What would our lives look like today if we didn't have the opportunities freedom has afforded us? If our path had been largely determined by some kind of dictator or despot? Very different, no doubt. And while none of us is ever entirely free from obligation and duty, we still enjoy the freedom to choose our relationships, jobs, and homes to some degree.

What privileges have you taken advantage of as a result of your freedoms ? How is your life continuing to be enriched by that "something in the air of America" that fills human souls with the breath of independence?

The rights we enjoy as North Americans have given us a significant measure of self-determination. Indeed, we have been blessed with considerable opportunities.

Prayer: God, may I ever be grateful for the tremendous opportunities I enjoy within the country you've given me.

❧ ❧ ❧ ❧

ENCOURAGING OTHERS WITH GRATITUDE

* * * *

THANKFUL FOR HIS BLINDNESS

Those who are grateful in adversity inspire others to be more grateful.

Verse for the Day: "Do not let the downtrodden be put to shame; let the poor and needy praise your name" (Psa 74:21).

AT A CHURCH IN BOSTON, an English minister was called upon one Sunday to fill the pulpit for Dr. Phillips Brooks. After the service, intending to return to his hotel, he realized that he didn't know the way. He then turned to the man standing behind him and inquired about directions back to the hotel.

"Why, you're the minister I just heard. I'm blind, but I can show you the way. I can take you to the door."

Not wanting to inconvenience the man, the minister assured him he needn't accompany him. However, the volunteer guide persisted, "You will not refuse me the pleasure of helping you? I so seldom have the opportunity to render service. Everyone is so kind to me."

As the men walked to the hotel, the blind man said, "I live alone. I can go about the streets without a guide. I am thankful for my blindness because I have so much time for quiet meditation. There will be time enough in heaven for me to see everything!"

How those words must have rung in the minister's ears that day! A man whose sight was gone, no doubt, inspired everyone he met to become a little more grateful and to look for the blessings in life's challenges.

Prayer: God, while others count their blessings despite difficulties, they inspire me to count mine as well.

* * * *

THE CAMPAIGN FOR THANKSGIVING DAY
Celebrating our blessings together encourages us to be grateful.

Verse for the Day: "Enter his gates with thanksgiving, and his courts with praise. Give thanks to him, bless his name. For the Lord is good; his steadfast love endures forever, and his faithfulness to all generations" (Psa 100:4–5).

WE OWE A DEBT of gratitude to Sarah Hale, the woman who was primarily responsible for the national institution of Thanksgiving Day in the United States. Although the Pilgrims celebrated the first

Thanksgiving in 1621, few people realize that Thanksgiving became a national holiday in the middle of the twentieth century.

After the United States became a nation, President Washington issued a Thanksgiving Day Proclamation in 1789. Thomas Jefferson, however, regarded it with disdain and officially ended it after he became president. Subsequently, some states observed Thanksgiving, arbitrarily selecting their own dates for the event.

Several years later, Sarah Hale became the editor of the magazine *Godey's Lady's Book*. In 1828, she then sought to restore Thanksgiving as a national holiday. After many years of being rejected and ignored by government officials, Hale finally found an audience with President Lincoln in 1863. Following her plea for the North and South to "lay aside enmities and strife on [Thanksgiving] Day," Lincoln was so moved that he proclaimed the fourth Thursday of November the official national Thanksgiving Day. Nevertheless, it was not until 1941 that the U.S. Congress ratified this day of celebration.

We have Sarah Hale to thank for persisting in her quest for a national observance of Thanksgiving. And next Thanksgiving, as we gather with family and friends to remember all that we have to be grateful for, we can include a word of thanks for the gathering time itself in our prayers.

Prayer: God, though we have the wonderful opportunity to thank you each day for your blessings, it is especially good to have a special day for gathering to express our gratitude together.

* * * *

A LITTLE GRATITUDE GOES A LONG WAY
**Our little expressions of thanks
can have a big impact on others.**

Verse for the Day: "Let the peace of Christ rule in your hearts.... And be thankful" (Col 3:15).

SEVERAL DECADES AGO the army sent a soldier to a rest camp after a long stretch of active duty. When this soldier rejoined his platoon, he took a few moments to write a letter to General George Patton, thanking him for the needed rest he enjoyed at the camp. Replying to that letter, Patton informed him that for 35 years he had done his best for his soldiers as a commanding officer. Patton then said his letter was the only time one of his soldiers had thanked him during his entire career with the U.S. army.

Sometimes we underestimate the significance of our simple expressions of thanks. Certainly, some of our gratitude will fall to the ground, little noticed. Yet we never know when a note or word of appreciation to someone, whose efforts we have been helped by, might be the first they've heard in a long time—or perhaps the first ever!

A little gratitude can go a long way toward encouraging those who are giving something of themselves to us. And often, just that bit of affirmation that their efforts are not being wasted gives them that little lift they need to keep going.

Prayer: God, please remind me to express my thanks to others, and by it may many be blessed and encouraged.

* * * *

THE RETURNS OF GRATITUDE
My expressions of gratitude motivate others to continue doing good things.

Verse for the Day: "Let us consider how to provoke one another to love and good deeds" (Heb 10:24).

THE YOUTH GROUP WAS PUTTING the finishing touches on sprucing up the Jenkins's yard. The elderly couple had been finding it difficult to keep up with the demands of their lawn, shrubs, and flowerbeds during the summer months. When all of the necessary tasks were completed, Mr. Jenkins called the kids to the front porch for lemonade and cookies. The troop of dirty-faced, tired teens gratefully accepted the refreshments.

"Kids," Mr. Jenkins announced and cleared his throat, "Mrs. Jenkins and I want to thank each of you. You've done a great job, and we're thrilled you've come to help us out."

The young people responded with the chatter of their individual "you're welcomes." Everyone was smiling and enjoying the mutual gratification of having given and having received.

The next week, the kids were back, and the next week, and the next. All summer long, the Jenkins enjoyed the weekend visits from the yard-crew youths who were energized and inspired by the expressions of appreciation they received from this loving senior couple.

Prayer: God, today grant me opportunities to show my gratefulness to others for their kindnesses, knowing that as I do, blessings will flow in both directions.

* * * *

HOPE
HOPE GIVES US A BETTER TODAY

• • • •

JOYFUL SINGING BRINGS HOPE

Optimism that springs from hope brings enjoyment to each day.

Verse for the Day: "This is the day that the Lord has made; let us rejoice and be glad in it" (Psa 118:24).

A TELEVISION SITCOM that was popular in the seventies featured two women, Laverne and Shirley, who were best friends, sharing an apartment in Milwaukee, Wisconsin. As blue-collar workers, their lifestyle was simple, and their existence rather mundane. Yet they lived in a constant state of optimism and anticipation of what the day might bring.

They would often sing about hope, and faithful viewers could always sense a song coming whenever Laverne sat dejected on the sofa and Shirley wrapped an arm around her friend's shoulders and began swaying back and forth. Then they would begin to sing together, and soon Laverne would again believe that life was good and that she could successfully meet whatever challenges had earlier seemed so daunting.

Of course, sitcoms are not real life, but hope *is* real. In fact, it's not an oversimplification of reality to say that hope—the optimism with which we face whatever the day brings—can give us the ability to rejoice and be glad in every day.

Prayer: It's a blessing to have a new day full of potential, God. Grant me the optimism, the hope, to face it with gladness.

* * * *

Daily Reminders to Hope
Our dreams can be kept alive by daily reminders to reach for them.

Verse for the Day: "Be strong, and let your heart take courage, all you who wait for the Lord" (Psa 31:24).

LILY LIKES TO DREAM. A while back she had a fanciful idea and related it over the phone to her sister, Emma, who lives several hundred miles away in another state.

"Wouldn't it be a lot of fun," Lily asked, "to be able to buy an old, honest-to-goodness lighthouse and turn it into a bed-and-breakfast?"

Emma, who is a wonderful hostess, found the idea appealing and quickly joined her sister in a detour through this dream world. After a thorough talking out of the possibilities, the sisters left the topic with, "Well, who knows? Maybe someday."

Several months later, Emma, who lives on the Oregon coast, was talking again on the phone to Lily and asked, "Remember that bed-and-breakfast idea you had? Well, I saw one—a lighthouse. It was quite nice."

"So it can be done," laughed Lily. "Well, maybe one day we'll just do it ourselves."

At Christmas time, a gift was delivered to Lily. It was from Emma. After Lily opened the box and dug through the Styrofoam, she pulled out a present that needed no explanation. It was a little stained-glass lighthouse with a stand from which it could hang.

Today, the lighthouse sits in front of the window in Lily's kitchen. Several times a day, she sees her sister's reminder of their far-fetched, but not impossible idea. Whenever Lily sees the sun illuminating the colors of the glass, her hope is nudged a little, and her dream is kept alive.

Prayer: God, thank you for brightening my day with reminders of hope and encouragement of dreams.

* * * *

HOPE FLOATS...
ON THE NILE
Today's signs of hope are food for the soul.

*Verse for the Day: "But I will hope continually,
and will praise you yet more and more"* (Psa 71:14).

*A*N OLD RABBINICAL LEGEND tells a story from ancient Egypt during the time when Joseph (one of
Jacob's 12 sons) had been made second in command to
Pharaoh. A seven-year famine had struck the land, but
prior to its occurrence, Joseph had overseen the careful
storage of grains so that there was plenty of food in
Egypt.

According to the legend, during the famine, Joseph
ordered that the chaff in his granaries be thrown into
the Nile river. While the chaff floated along the river's
currents, the people watched from the banks from far
away. Although it was only chaff, it indicated that there
was an abundance of corn in the granaries.

As the people observed the floating chaff, they were
certain that they would receive the food they needed.
They needed only to have enough strength to get to
where the chaff was being dumped into the Nile.

Signs of hope are like that. The sign itself, like the chaff on the Nile, may be insignificant, but its implication can be wonderful news that nourishes our soul with courage and strength to move ahead. Sometimes it takes careful observation to see the signs of hope around us, but they're there if we'll look for them. And when we let ourselves think about all that they imply, we discover that the day is full of new promise.

Prayer: God, as you open my eyes to the signs of hope all around me, let me draw new courage and strength from them.

. . . .

A Full Supply of Hope
As long as there is hope,
there is no surrender to despair.

Verse for the Day: "Hope in God; for I shall again praise him, my help and my God" (Psa 42:5).

A Scottish castle under siege by invading enemy forces had held out for a very long time. As the weeks wore on with no surrender, the enemy was certain that the castle's inhabitants had to be near death with no food left to sustain them. It was with an air of victory that the attackers sent a message, insisting on immediate surrender.

The invaders' confidence was short lived, however, for much to their dismay, they soon saw a fantastic display of fresh-caught fish dangling down the castle wall. The people within were not starving—they were feasting! They had access to an underground waterway to the sea from which they could catch all the food they needed.

Hope springs eternal—so the adage goes. And for these Scots, their spring of hope was their supply of fish. As long as they had food and water, their enemies would be waiting a very long time to defeat them.

What is your supply of hope today to keep the enemy of despair from coming near your fortress? A commitment to optimism? A goal you're determined to reach? Strong relationships with family and friends? Or the most plentiful of sources—a strong faith in God?

Whatever your supply of hope, go to it often. Keep your soul full of its goodness. And if someone tries to bring a message of discouragement, throw a string of hope over the wall to remind them that you're not planning to give up any time soon.

Prayer: Gracious God, keep my soul full of the bountiful hope you supply each day.

*   *   *   *

HOPE GIVES US A BRIGHTER TOMORROW

* * * *

THE DAY WILL COME

When we are certain of what we hope for, we know our hope will be rewarded in time.

Verse for the Day: "But if we hope for what we do not see, we wait for it with patience" (Rom 8:25).

REMEMBER WHEN YOU WERE A KID, and Christmas was just a week away? That one week seemed to stretch out longer than the previous months that made up the year. The waiting was agonizing, but it was also exciting because you knew there was a special gift just for you, waiting to be unwrapped.

As we've become older, we've learned to enjoy the weeks and days leading up to Christmas almost as much as the event itself. Why? Because we've learned to wait patiently for what will come, realizing there's even joy in waiting. Similarly, as people who trust in God, we have come to understand that waiting for the fulfillment of God's promises to unfold in our lives is a process in which we can find joy. For we know that the time will come when our hope will be fully realized.

Of course, the kind of hope that paints a bright glow on the horizon of tomorrow is not the cross-your-fingers wishing of the gambler. No, that kind of hope is quickly and easily disappointed. Yet the kind of hope that excites children at Christmastime and fills believers in God with anticipation of the future is not a gamble. It is a certainty.

The brightly wrapped packages under the tree are promises, guaranteeing future fulfillment of the child's hope. Likewise, for those who trust God, his word and his promises for the future make our hope for an even brighter tomorrow certain beyond doubt.

Prayer: God, your promises fill me with hope and help me wait patiently for their fulfillment.

, , , ,

THE WAY OF HOPE
News that brings hope is like a breath of fresh air.

Verse for the Day: "The light of the eyes rejoices the heart, and good news refreshes the body" (Prov 15:30).

HAVE YOU EVER WONDERED HOW the southern tip of Africa got its name? It was, in fact, once called "Cape of Tempests," for it had a nasty reputation. Sailors dreaded making the swing around the great continent. And for good reason. The often-stormy waters devoured numerous ships and crews. A Portuguese navigator, however, made it his personal mission to find a less teacherous route and did so, effectively turning the Cape of Tempests into the Cape of Good Hope.

It's easy to imagine a scene from those earlier days of sea travel. Perhaps an old, seasoned sailor would describe the fierce waters ahead, as the vessel approached Africa's southern cape. Then laughing, the seafarer might say, "Aye, but that was before she was renamed 'Good Hope,' and now we sing as we sail 'round her."

Hope. It is that passage through the stormy waters. It is that wonderful good news that comes on the heels of the bad. It is what reminds us that all is not lost, that we can go on, and that tomorrow has much promise. Indeed, it is only hope that can give us the courage to whistle as we continue on our way.

What is the news of hope for you today? What is the good word that brings a sigh of relief to your soul? Speak it over and over again, and breathe it in like the air of a warm spring morning. Let hope refresh your body and spirit as you welcome its good message.

Prayer: God, overwhelm my spirit with hope today and place a song in my heart as I continue on my way.

❧ ❧ ❧ ❧

ULTIMATE HOPE
Ultimate hope for eternal life is cause for rejoicing.

Verse for the Day: "Now may our Lord Jesus Christ himself and God our Father, who loved us and through grace gave us eternal comfort and good hope, comfort your hearts and strengthen them in every good work and word" (2 Thess 2:16–17).

THE TWO SHORTEST VERSES in the King James Version of the Bible are these: "Jesus wept" (John 11:35) and "Rejoice evermore" (1 Thess 5:16). While the first of the two is the shortest in English, the second is actually the shorter of the two in the original Greek.

It has been noted that there is a connection to be seen between these two brief portions of Scripture. For Jesus' tears of compassion and sacrifice have brought about eternal rejoicing for those who will trust in him.

Within Jesus' warm embrace, we find our deepest desires met, our hopes realized, and our future secure. It is this fantastic certainty of hope out of which rejoicing can continually flow from our hearts.

Prayer: God, I trust in you for eternal life, and I rejoice in the certainty of that hope.

* * * *

THE HOPE OF PEACE

God has given us the hope of future peace in his eternal kingdom.

Verse for the Day: "Surely there is a future, and your hope will not be cut off" (Prov 23:18).

A LARGE BRONZE STATUE of a lion stands on the plains of Waterloo. The materials from which it was crafted came from the weapons of Britain's enemies in 1815. A man named Walter Baxendale once described it as he saw it one spring afternoon. He observed that the open, snarling mouth of the great lion held a delicate nest of baby birds. The nest was woven around the lion's menacing teeth, yet the new life in the nest rested peacefully there. Baxendale saw this scene as a symbol of great hope.

Hope, by its very nature, dares to thrive in the most unlikely of places. The hope for peace is no exception. Our world's history is littered with wars, great and small, and to this day, the great cauldron still boils with fighting and unrest. However, like those nestlings reposed in the mouth of the formidable-looking lion, God's children remain at peace in a world of human fury and strife. Why? Because of hope.

Yet our hope does not lie in humanity's ability to achieve the ideal of worldwide peace. It lies, rather, in God's promise to one day establish his kingdom of righteousness and peace. As we wait for God's timing to unfold, we can remain at rest in our souls because of our sure hope that God will bring about a peaceful future in which we will live forever.

Prayer: God, I continue to hope in your future kingdom of peace and righteousness.

* * * *

ENCOURAGING OTHERS WITH HOPE

* * * *

SHOOTING DOWN DOUBT

We can encourage hope in others by allaying their doubts.

~ஒ~

Verse for the Day: "For whatever was written in former days was written for our instruction, so that by steadfastness and by the encouragement of the scriptures we might have hope" (Rom 15:4).

WHILE I WAS STRUGGLING with a decision, wondering whether I was doing the right thing in moving toward my goal, a friend of mine said, "Something that has helped me over and over is remembering this: Never doubt in the darkness what God has shown you in the light."

That little bit of instruction has stayed with me as I've wrestled with self-doubt and discouragement on my way to pursuing the work I love to do—the work God created me to do. Time and again my friend's words have effectively shot down my doubts and encouraged me to trust in God's truth.

What tidbits of hope have you gathered over the years that have been effective in dissolving your uncertainty and in giving you courage to continue hoping? Perhaps a line from a movie or book, a verse of poetry, song, or Scripture, even an inspiring illustration from your experience. As you bring these to mind, don't forget that what has inspired you may well inspire others. Pass along some gems from your bank of inspiration. These doubt-busting, hope-building words that carried you through some rough spots will carry others through as well.

Prayer: God of hope, thank you that I can pass on to others the same words of inspiration you have given me to dispel my doubts.

❧ ❧ ❧ ❧

BEING AN AMBASSADOR OF HOPE

We can pass our hope along
to those whose hope is flagging.

Verse for the Day: "Now faith, hope, and love abide"
(1 Cor 13:13).

PERHAPS NEVER WAS THERE a more aptly named entertainer than Bob Hope. For nearly 50 years he used his gift of joke-telling to bring hope and cheer to military troops stationed in difficult situations around the globe.

Hope has entertained troops overseas in every war from World War II to the Gulf War. The news media has called him "America's #1 Soldier in Greasepaint," and the soldiers have dubbed him "G. I. Bob." Hope, as a messenger of cheer, began his "mission" in May of 1941 when he went with a group of Hollywood performers to March Field, California, to do a radio show for military personnel stationed there. His first trip into a combat area was in 1943 during World War II when he and a small group of USO entertainers encouraged troops in England, Africa, Sicily, and Iceland. In peacetime, Hope continued his visits to military bases and veterans' hospitals.

In 1948, Hope began his Christmas-show custom when he went to Germany to entertain military personnel who were involved in the Berlin airlift. Years later, in 1972, while doing a show for soldiers in Vietnam, Hope announced that this would be his last Christmas show. Contrary to his announcement, however, Hope continued year after year with his tradition of going wherever soldiers faced the lonely holidays far from loved ones.

Hope went to Beirut in 1983. Then in 1987, he flew around the world to the Pacific, Atlantic, and Indian oceans and then to the Persian Gulf. His Goodwill Tour in 1990 took him to England, Russia, and Germany. The tour's grand finale was in Saudi Arabia, where Hope offered his "cup of Christmas cheer" to the men and women of Operation Desert Storm.

Bob Hope, born on May 29, 1903, is well into his nineties now, but he continues to tell his jokes. Although he has recently retired from making his global treks to cheer the troops, there is no doubt that for years to come, he will remain an icon of hope to those whose lives he has touched.

Prayer: God, today let me be a messenger of hope and goodwill to the people in my life whose spirits may need a lift.

❧ ❧ ❧ ❧

ROOTING FOR THE UNDERDOG

Instilling hope in those who seem hopeless can have surprising results.

Verse for the Day: "For while we were still weak, at the right time Christ died for the ungodly" (Rom 5:6).

WHEN I WAS A CHILD, there was a cartoon character, a pathetic little pooch named Underdog, whose mission was to stick up for the little guys, the underdogs in life.

Underdogs are those seemingly hopeless cases that seem as if they'll never amount to anything: the football team that hasn't won a game all season; the scrawniest kid in gym class; the Cinderellas and Charlie Browns of life who are always being stepped on by someone with an advantage.

Yet underdogs have an uncanny way of coming out on top, and usually their victories are inspired by a ray of hope given to them by someone who is rooting for them. Underdog football teams, inspired by coaches and fans, have been known to upset heavy favorites. The scrawny kid in gym class often shows up at the class reunion, tall, dark, handsome, and successful—

and married to a woman who loved him before he got that way. Cinderella, with a little help from her fairy godmother, made it to the ball and won the prince's heart. Charlie Brown—well, who knows what could happen if he received a little more encouragement from his friends?

Meanwhile, if there's an underdog you know of who could use a ray of hope, you have an opportunity to be that person's inspiration. But be warned: You might end up hearing your name mentioned on national television as they thank you for making them what they are today.

Prayer: Just as you have encouraged me with hope, God, may I encourage those who seem to be without hope.

❧ ❧ ❧ ❧

HUMOR

HUMOR REVEALS THE
LIGHTER SIDE OF LIFE

* * * *

SMILING AT THE PAST

Looking into the past can reveal interesting,
amusing, and fun history.

*Verse for the Day: "When I was a child, I spoke like a child,
I thought like a child, I reasoned like a child"* (1 Cor 13:11).

A PEEK INTO THE PAST can reveal tidbits that can
make us smile. One amusing story dates back a
century in the town of Evanston, Illinois (nicknamed
"Heavenston" for the religious zeal of its citizens).

The town officials were concerned about the fountain
store's effects on piety. To curb patronage to these
stores on Sunday, these leaders made it a regulation
that no ice cream sodas could be sold on that day.

Complying with the ordinance, but having the savvy to
sidestep it, some of the fountain owners successfully
promoted a new dessert; ice cream served with a fla-
vored syrup but with no soda. It was called the "Sunday
soda" and was a favorite with many customers.

When the popular treat was ordered on weekdays, a number of people voiced opposition to its being named for the Lord's day. In compliance with this concern, the spelling was changed and has remained as the dessert we know today as the ice cream sundae.

History is full of interesting and humorous events. Even our personal history has its laughable moments. Reading books about the lighter side of history and reflecting on our own misconceptions, foibles, and silly mistakes can enliven our day with laughter.

Prayer: God, thank you for the funny side of life that is often seen more clearly in hindsight.

* * * *

REMINDING OTHERS TO LAUGH

Our sense of humor can help others remember to enjoy life.

Verse for the Day: "A glad heart makes a cheerful countenance" (Prov 15:13).

MANY YEARS AGO, hunching over my geometry book at my grandparents' house, I was frustrated by my inability to solve some of the assigned problems. The crumbs from my eraser were building up on the tablecloth with each new attempt at a solution.

While I rested my head on my book in defeat, I felt a gentle tap on my shoulder. Turning around in my chair, my eyes were drawn to a little, white jewelry box my grandpa was extending to me.

"What's this?" I asked in surprise.

"Oh, it's just a little something for you," he said modestly. "Actually, it's a diamond pin," he disclosed.

"For me?" I must have looked incredulous.

"Well, don't get too excited until you see it," he said.

As I gingerly opened the lid and pulled back a layer of cotton, I was saying, "Grandpa, diamonds are too expens—" but I stopped short. Lying tucked in the fluffy cotton was a safety pin on which was glued a dime.

"You see," Grandpa declared, "it's a dime-and-pin! And you can tell all your friends you have one."

As we laughed together, I pinned the gag gift on my shirt and enjoyed the much-needed gift of humor Grandpa had interjected into my evening.

Prayer: I'm grateful to you, God, for the gift of humor that allows me to laugh and lifts the spirits of others as well.

❧ ❧ ❧ ❧

PEOPLE ARE FUNNY

Life is more entertaining because people are amusing.

Verse for the Day: "The heart of fools is in the house of mirth" (Eccl 7:4).

AT A HOLLYWOOD PARTY, Greta Garbo struck up a conversation with Albert Einstein. She knew little of his work, but enough to ask, "I understand you have a great theory. Won't you please explain it all to me?"

"My dear lady," Einstein replied, "I'm afraid there will not be enough time to explain the theory of relativity, but perhaps I can tell you about the law of gravitation."

Einstein then explained gravity and its effects to her. When he was through, the movie star was so fascinated that she exclaimed, "Well, for goodness's sake, Doctor, how long has this been going on?"

People are funny. And each of us is part of that funny "collective" because from time to time, each of us says or does something that can be deemed amusing. Yet it is precisely our funnyness—our foibles and goof-ups—that makes life a little more entertaining.

Because we all play the fool from time to time, it's a wonderful gift to ourself and others when we have the grace to laugh at our silly mistakes. It's also a blessing when, rather than mock others, we can ease their embarrassment and help them laugh at themselves when their moment of infamy comes.

As long as there are people, there will be foolishness—however unintentional. And as long as we can laugh at ourselves, life will be a little lighter, a little more fun because of it.

Prayer: God, how fallible we are and how much we need the grace to make light of our harmless, honest mistakes.

, , , ,

HUMOR ENERGIZES US

, , , ,

LAUGH HEARTILY, LAUGH OFTEN

Humor helps us reap the healthful benefits of laughter.

Verse for the Day: "Our mouth was filled with laughter, and our tongue with shouts of joy" (Psa 126:2).

I S LAUGHTER REALLY the best medicine? The answer to this question is certainly open to debate. Yet some modern medical studies have uncovered evidence that indicates laughter is an agent of health.

Some of its positive mental, emotional, and physical effects include stimulating endorphins, which numb physical pain; producing an energy "rush" that results in relaxation; brightening one's mood; reducing stress, fear, and anxiety; breaking down relational barriers; and building trust between people. That's quite an impressive range of benefits! And, as an added bonus, there are no negative side effects to this wonder drug.

Individuals who make laughter a regular part of their day experience the full advantage of its powers. We can make laughter a routine part of our lives as well by indulging in fun and positive humor on a daily basis. (Note: Sarcasm, put-downs, and other such negative "humor" are not of the healthful variety.)

By reading the work of humorous writers in books, magazines, and newspapers—including favorite comic strips; by watching movies or television programs that make us laugh; by hearing and telling funny jokes; by spending time with friends whose sense of humor we enjoy; by these and other such laugh-inducing methods, we can become healthier and happier. And all without receiving a single bill from the doctor's office!

What tickles your funny bone? Be good to yourself today and make sure you get a good dose of whatever that is. Remind yourself to laugh daily. You might even go so far as to add a bottle with a label that says "laughter" to your arsenal of vitamins or to write "laugh" on your list of things to do each day.

It really doesn't matter how you choose to remember that you need to laugh, the important thing is that you find a way to make it happen. Keep in mind that each time you laugh, you're taking care of your health, and by doing that, you'll be experiencing a new level of enjoyment in life.

Prayer: God, fill my mouth with laughter and my heart with joy.

*H*EEEERE'S *D*OTTY!
Friends who help us laugh energize our lives.

Verse for the Day: "A cheerful heart is a good medicine" (Prov 17:22).

O*N* S*UNDAY* MORNINGS, a small group of seniors gathers at a table in the refreshment area at their community church. As they sip coffee and nibble pastries, they exchange post-worship conversation. All goes quietly along until . . .

Enter Dotty. Her entire persona exudes humor and fun. The group livens at her appearance, and their voices raise to give her a worthy greeting.

"Hi, kids!" she quips. "Leave any for me?" and looks with mock longing at a muffin. Even her brightly colored clothing communicates a zest for life. And everyone—young and old—loves Dotty.

It seems we all know someone like Dotty, someone who can raise spirits and bring smiles just by walking into a room. Such people are a gift to us. Indeed, they bring our level of enjoyment to a higher plane and infuse our days with energy and laughter. They are a virtual medicine for our souls.

Prayer: God, as I think about people who energize me with their humor, I'm grateful for their presence in my life.

* * * *

HUMOR FOR DESSERT?
**Laughing together with friends
and family is a treat for the soul.**

*Verse for the Day: "A cheerful heart has
a continual feast"* (Prov 15:15).

CELEBRATING MY MOM'S 54TH BIRTHDAY was a peaceful and (quite honestly) rather uneventful get-together. Grandma, my brother and his family, and, of course, my dad, all came to wish Mom happiness. After lunch, there was conversation, some televised football, and cake. By late afternoon, we were all feeling really lethargic.

This party needs a pick-me-up, I thought. I knew some humor would do the trick, but being the not-so-creative hostess, I couldn't think of a way to personally rally the troops. So I did the only thing that came to mind: I powered up the VCR and popped in a videotape of a Bill Cosby stand-up comedy performance.

As the tape rolled, so did we—practically on the floor. As Grandma laughed at Cosby's witty child-rearing anecdotes, she told me, "I've seen this once before with your grandpa. He about fell out of his chair laughing." I could imagine my grandfather getting a kick out of Cosby, and I smiled. *It's a treat to laugh together with these people I've gone through life with,* I thought.

It's true. Humor has the power to draw people together, lift our spirits, and create memorable moments. Sharing laughter with those we love leaves a sweetness in our souls to savor for a lifetime.

Prayer: God, I relish the "dessert" of laughter I share with my family and friends.

＊　＊　＊　＊

Humor Helps Us See the Truth

. . . .

The Gentle Nudge of Wit

Wit can be a gentle prompt to help
others take necessary action.

Verse for the Day: "Speaking the truth in love" (Eph 4:15).

*H*UMOR HAS THE UNCANNY ABILITY to soften a
rebuke while at the same time making its point
more poignant than a direct admonishment. For example, as an editor on a Missouri newspaper, Mark Twain
received a letter from a subscriber, who noted that he
had discovered a spider crawling in his newspaper
copy. The subscriber asked if this indicated good or
bad luck. Twain replied:

"Old Subscriber: Finding a spider in your paper was
neither good luck nor bad luck for you. The spider was
merely looking over our paper to see which merchant
is not advertising so that he can go to that store, spin
his web across the door, and lead a life of undisturbed
peace ever afterward."

The merchants at whom this good-natured jab was
directed had to chuckle at Twain's wit, despite the sting
of his message to them. It would be interesting to know

how many of them heeded the implicit warning by taking out their first advertisement in his newspaper.

While Twain's not-so-underlying motives were to bring in advertising dollars to his newspaper, he effectively used his sense of humor to get across his message in a lighthearted manner.

As we exercise our wit with love and discretion, we can gently help others see truth they might not have listened to by any other approach. In a very real sense, wit can point someone in the right direction and give them the nudge they need to get going.

Prayer: God, grant me wisdom as I use wit to lovingly impart truth to those who might need to hear it.

. . . .

COMIC RELIEF
Comedy helps us look at the truth about ourselves in a nonthreatening way.

Verse for the Day: "To make an apt answer is a joy to anyone, and a word in season, how good it is!" (Prov 15:23).

A GOOD NUMBER OF COMEDIANS make their living using a verbal tool literary folks call hyperbole—an exaggeration of reality. With this little device, stand-up comics, script producers, and humor writers alike can cast human tendency, shortcoming, and idiosyncrasy in a funny light.

Audiences laugh at these magnified and overblown reflections of life precisely because they recognize themselves in the ridiculous picture that is painted for them. Much as we recognize a cartoon caricature of a famous person because there remains an element of truth in the artist's rendering, so we see ourselves in the comedian's portrayal of typical human attitudes and behavior.

Ah, the truth may hurt at other times and in other settings, but somehow in the couch of comedy, we can more readily accept the truth of how silly our pride is and how laughable our thinking and actions can be. Humor has the grace to slip us bits of truth without placing us on trial, which makes it easier for us to make changes.

For all of the reasons mentioned above, the term "comic relief" is an apt one. Perhaps a final element of the relief comedy provides is that it helps us know that we are not alone. When an entire roomful of people laughs at the same joke, it is highly likely that they are laughing for the same reasons. We all struggle, we all mess up, we all need to make changes, and we all need to laugh at ourselves once in a while in the whole process.

As from time to time, we take a look at the truth about ourselves through the eyes of comedy, we will find the relief of laughter and a bit of friendly insight to guide us along our way.

Prayer: God, thank you for humor that helps me laugh at myself and at the same time gives me new insight.

. . . .

Humor Smooths Things Over

Using humor creatively can help smooth over the mistakes of others.

Verse for the Day: "The Lord's servant must not be quarrelsome but kindly to everyone, an apt teacher, patient" (2 Tim 2:24).

*A*FTER MOVING ACROSS THE COUNTRY when her company promoted and relocated her, a woman wanted to find a new church home. Finally, after months of trying different churches, she found one she liked. Although she attended services for several weeks, she thought it strange and awkward that no one had attempted to contact her since she had indicated that she would welcome a visit on a visitor's response card.

Not wanting to fill out another response card that would be ignored, the woman thought of another way to establish contact. After she wrote out her check for the offering plate, she tore it in half and wrote the following on the half that had her name and address printed on it: "Someone can come to my home to pick up the other half of this check. I'm new in town and would very much like to get to know you and learn more about the church's ministries." She smiled as she dropped it into the offering plate.

That week, a team of visitors sheepishly knocked on her door. Everyone had a good laugh, and all was forgiven as they introduced themselves and enjoyed one another's company.

Such creative and witty responses to our frustrations with others are far better than lashing out in anger. It is a gracious person who offers a rebuke softened with comic relief when others fail them. Humor has the ability to allow people to laugh together at their shortcomings and oversights, smoothing over rough spots in relationships, offering a unique brand of kindness.

Prayer: When it is appropriate, God, use my humor to smooth over the rough spots in my relationships.

✽ ✽ ✽ ✽

Joy

THE JOY OF GOOD RELATIONSHIPS

. . . .

THE JOY OF A GOOD MARRIAGE

A shared lifetime of mutual
respect and love is an abiding joy.

*Verse for the Day: "If one offered for love all the wealth of
one's house, it would be utterly scorned" (Sol 8:7).*

WHEN GEORGE BURNS and Gracie Allen met, they
were two vaudeville performers just trying to
make ends meet. Gracie was looking for a partner for
an act, and George, always looking for a performance
angle, was game to try something new.

As far as romance, neither had an initial interest in the
other. George wasn't a candidate for marriage; he was
enjoying the freedom of playing the field. Gracie wasn't
interested in George; she was in love with another man.
As they worked together, however, George first became
intrigued by and then fell in love with Gracie. His
toughest challenge, it seemed, was trying to convince
Miss Allen of his love for her.

Gracie wasn't easily won. She could not believe that George, the ladies' man, could be serious about a relationship, and there was also the matter of the other man she believed she would eventually marry.

It took some doing, but George finally persuaded Gracie to marry him. Together they adopted and raised two children—a girl and a boy—while working successfully together on stage, in radio, and eventually on television.

While Gracie was by far the more popular of the two during their heyday, George didn't mind. He just loved working with her and being her best friend and cheerleader. Gracie, in turn, valued George's input into their professional endeavors and drew strength and comfort from his reassuring presence. Gracie's persistent fear of being in front of a microphone or an audience was often relieved when she felt George's hand on her shoulder as they performed their comedy routines.

Tender consideration for each other characterized their married life together. Because Gracie never wore short sleeves in public, few people knew that she had a badly burned left arm from a childhood accident. Gracie was self-conscious of the disfigurement, and one time, as she and George were lying in bed rehearsing lines for a performance, Gracie put down her script and said, "You know, Nattie [what she called George], the nicest thing you've ever done for me is that you never said anything about my bad arm." To which George replied, "Oh, really? Which arm is the bad arm?"

The couple shared a unique relationship, working together rather than competing, sharing their ups and downs rather than boasting or blaming, encouraging one another rather than tearing down. Such friendships—especially in marriage—cast a unique light of joy that even the shadow of time cannot extinguish.

Prayer: I offer my praise to you, God, each time the joy of close relationships you've granted sheds its light into my day.

• • • •

A GRANDPARENT'S JOY
Grandparenting brings unique joy to my life.

Verse for the Day: Grandchildren are the crown to the aged (Prov 17:6).

ALTHOUGH JIM IS RETIRED, he keeps quite busy with a postretirement business venture. It's not unusual to see him hurrying to the next appointment in his tight schedule.

Nevertheless, whenever one of Jim's grandchildren approaches him and begins a sentence with, "Grandpa, will you. . .?" he can't help but stop and at least listen to the request. After having raised his own children, Jim realizes that these "inconveniences" are really precious opportunities in disguise.

Such interruptions may lead to anything from helping with a potty break to giving little boys and girls a ride in one of his large tractors. Yet Jim will tell you that few things in life compare with the pure joy he experiences in spending these moments with his grandchildren.

Prayer: God, thank you for the joy I receive in being a grandparent and for each opportunity I have to spend time with my grandchildren.

* * * *

THE JOY OF LOVE'S WELCOME

Wherever we are welcomed with love, there is joy.

~⊗~

Verse for the Day: "Better is a dinner of vegetables where love is than a fatted ox and hatred with it" (Prov 15:17).

A PAINTING BY M. ANTHONY, entitled "The Return from Labor," displays a beautiful landscape of striking colors portraying the evening sky, the gathering of clouds at twilight, and cattle sleeping in the fields. Yet the focus in the painting is the three people who greet each other with love and joy.

A man is trudging home after a hard day's work. Though he is no doubt weary, his countenance is animated with delight, for he has just caught sight of his wife. She is holding their young child and has come outside to welcome him home. The depiction of their mutual love and happiness is, indeed, the supreme beauty of the work.

Clearly the beauty of loving relationships outshines all other earthly beauties, and the joy we experience as we feel the welcoming warmth of family and friends has no parallel. Our grandchildren running to us with outstretched arms, our children wanting us to hear their latest news, our spouse holding us in a tender embrace, our friends lighting up with happiness as we enter the room, and even the friendly hellos of those who would seek our acquaintance: These are love's welcome, life's chief treasures that fill our hearts with joy again and again.

Prayer: God, thank you for love's welcome that invites me into its beauty and gives me such indescribable joy.

* * * *

THE JOY OF MEMORIES

. . . .

TREASURING SACRED MEMORIES

Remembering special events in our lives provides a sense of joy.

Verse for the Day: "Mary treasured all these words and pondered them in her heart" (Luke 2:19).

FROM TIME TO TIME I read this poem: "Deep cuts in living marble— / Birthing room / Bride and groom / Silent Wake— / Made smooth again / By days between." When I come across this poem, I'm reminded that the everydayness of life can wear smooth my memory of significant events.

Of course, time can be a blessed healer, relieving us of the sting of painful memories. Yet what about when time stealthily erodes the sense of awe or elation or love we've felt toward God, family, or friends during a birth, wedding, or anniversary? How easy it seems to let the joy of those shared, sacred moments evaporate into the past!

Is there a way to retain the warmth of our memories? Happily, yes. Mary, Jesus' mother, knew how to hold onto her most treasured memories—the events surrounding Jesus' birth and infancy—and we can take our cues from her. Times of simple reflection can help bring back some of the magic. And in this modern age of photographs and video cameras, we have some added advantages for treasuring the joy of our most sacred memories.

Prayer: As I consider my life, God, I realize that I have been blessed by special experiences with others and with you—memories I can always treasure.

* * * *

REMEMBERING TOGETHER
Reminiscing with my family and long-time friends gives us joy and brings us closer together.

~◈~

Verse for the Day: "Remember the days of old, consider the years long past" (Deut 32:7).

"DO YOU REMEMBER THE TIME we took the long walk into town, and your neighbor's dog followed us the whole way?" I asked Grandma.

"Yes! And you know, I paid for a collar and leash when we were in town so we could get him home safely, and guess what?" Grandma queried.

"What?" I asked, though I knew the answer. (It's all part of our ritual.)

"That dumb dog got hit by a car just a few days later!" Grandma finished.

"Wouldn't you know it!" I declared, as I had the last time we'd visited the subject, and the time before.

Reminiscing with Grandma is one of my favorite family activities. Neither of us tires of hashing and rehashing "the good ole days." I enjoy a special closeness with my grandma, partly, I think, because of this very thing.

Memories are old maps that show where our paths have intersected on the journey. Memories are intangible but everlasting cords that draw us back to the places where they are anchored, reminding us that we are linked together, though we may reside miles apart. Time cannot rob us of these places in our experience, and when we revisit them again and again with those we love, we can develop a comforting closeness that brings unique joy to our relationships.

Prayer: Dear God, as I reminisce with friends and family about the times we've spent together, it gives me joy to realize anew how precious are my relationships with them.

❦ ❦ ❦ ❦

MEMORIES ARE FOR KEEPS

No matter what else may happen,
memories are a joy we can keep.

*Verse for the Day: "I consider the days of old,
and remember the years of long ago"* (Psa 77:5).

BERNICE AND VERONA WERE remembering Christmas traditions from their childhood. Both women, now in their seventies, could recall special traditions.

"I remember that my dad would send me all over the house," Bernice laughed. "He'd have a note that told me to look in the coal bin in the basement. Then a note in the coal bin would send me to the attic. I went all over that house until I'd finally find my special present in a closet or back behind the Christmas tree. One year it was a pair of leather riding boots. Oh, was I excited!"

Verona said what she remembered most was her family's tree-cutting tradition. Unlike Bernice's family, who lived in the city, Verona and her family had been farm folks and could hike into the nearby forest and choose a tree to cut down. Verona's voice lowered as she related a particularly meaningful tree-cutting event. "One time, just my brother and I got to go and choose the tree. It was snowy, and I remember we had a fun time together." A number of years later, Verona's brother was killed in a hunting accident. "I have that memory, though," she said, "and it came to mean a great deal to me after he was gone."

"That's the thing about memories," Bernice said. "Just as George Gershwin's famous lyrics say—they can take everything away from us, but they can't take our memories. We have those for keeps."

Prayer: God, I relish the joyful memories you have granted me through the years.

▪ ▪ ▪ ▪

FINDING JOY
IN THE DAY AND CREATION

▪ ▪ ▪ ▪

THE JOY OF SPRINGTIME
Springtime's promise of new life
fills our being with joyful anticipation.

*Verse for the Day: "The flowers appear on the earth;
the time of singing has come" (Sol 2:12).*

Now that Irene is in her later years, she often takes walks by a wooded acreage near her home. During early spring mornings, the damp air is always heavy with sweet springtime fragrances, and she likes to breathe deeply and close her eyes, trying to fully enjoy the blessing of spring's aroma.

Meanwhile, Irene also hears the calls and answers of the now-returned birds. She smiles and wonders what exactly they are saying to each other.

On sunny spring mornings Irene checks to see if the soft pussy willows have emerged from their branches. When they finally show their fuzzy faces, she breaks off a branch and tucks the buds into her pockets. She loves to feel them and imagines they are tiny, plump kittens.

In other seasons, while riding with her adult children to their place of worship, Irene never pays attention to the avenue of cherry trees that lines one of the streets in town. In springtime, however, she holds her breath as she looks out the car window at the canopy of blossoms that have suddenly appeared like Cinderella in her ball gown.

As the signs of springtime meet our senses in varied ways, we're reminded that freshness and newness are a part of our heritage as inhabitants of God's earth. Springtime's extravaganza shouts to our spirit, "Indeed, the season of singing has come!"

Prayer: God, you renew the earth in the springtime and renew my joy with its beauty.

❦   ❦   ❦   ❦

THE JOY OF SUMMERTIME
Summer's warmth and sunshine
bring the joy of optimism and activity.

Verse for the Day: "In the heavens he has set a tent for the sun, which comes out like a bridegroom from his wedding canopy, and like a strong man runs its course with joy" (Psa 19:4–5).

SUMMERTIME IS characterized by its warmth, by longer days, and by sunshine—wonderful sunshine!

Some scientific studies have shown a correlation between a positive state of mind and sunny weather. Of course, conventional wisdom has been aware of that relationship! Study or no study, summer holds the promise of picnics, fresh air, and warm starry nights. Crickets and fireflies, bullfrogs and hummingbirds are all a part of the celebration of the sun's glorious reign.

The blessings of summer encourages us to be optimistic about life. For the sunshine without creates sunshine within, and we eagerly and joyfully turn our faces to it like the splendid summer flowers.

Prayer: God, the summer sunshine reminds me that your presence is the sun in my soul, bringing warmth and joy.

᛭ ᛭ ᛭ ᛭

THE JOY OF AUTUMN'S BOUNTY

Autumn is a time to rejoice in and share the abundance of God's provisions.

Verse for the Day: "You crown the year with your bounty; your wagon tracks overflow with richness" (Psa 65:11).

*A*S AN ASPIRING JOURNALIST, Donald was always searching out stories for the campus newspaper. When he heard that one of the college's popular professors, Miss Dunbury, had recently returned from a trip to Romania (still in the years of the Cold War), he requested an interview with her.

In Miss Dunbury's office, Donald listened as the professor described her rewarding experience. She had traveled to Romania, having heard of that country's need for basic medical care. So she and others had carried aspirin and other such medicines into the country to distribute them among the people.

As she had gone about her work, Miss Dunbury had noticed long lines of people who waited hoping to purchase some small portion of meat to bring home to their families. Meat in Romania was a rare and prized commodity. "How very different from my life at home!" the elderly professor had noted.

Not long after returning to North America, Miss Dunbury made a trip to the supermarket. She shopped somewhat in a daze as she tried to adjust to the contrast between what she had just experienced in Romania and the vast number of items in the store. She told Donald that when she came to the meat cooler, her emotions were suddenly overwhelmed by the realization of the daily privileges she enjoyed in her homeland.

"Enjoy your good fortune in this country, Donald," the professor challenged. "It's a wonderful thing. Don't take it for granted, and share it whenever you can."

Each year, as autumn's bountiful provisions stock supermarkets, cupboards, and pantries, Donald remembers that interview and realizes with gratefulness the new opportunity he has to rejoice in his good fortune and to share some of the overflow of it.

Prayer: God, when I think of your provisions for me, I can't help but be joyful and express my gratitude to you by sharing with others.

* * * *

THE JOY OF
WINTER HOLIDAYS

**Winter holds the special joy
of celebrating holidays with others.**

*Verse for the Day: "Rejoice and exult
with all your heart"* (Zeph 3:14).

D O YOU REMEMBER your favorite New Year's celebration? Cheryl does. On her most memorable
New Year, she didn't count down the final seconds of
the old year with college friends. Rather, Aunt Margaret
had invited Cheryl over to spend a quiet evening.

Cheryl doesn't remember what she and her aunt
watched on TV that night as they put together a
1,500-piece jigsaw puzzle and drank sparkling cider.
What Cheryl does remember is just being silly with
Aunt Margaret, which transformed a simple observance into a night to remember.

Cheryl now knows that serendipitous moments lie in
wait at any given turn. For joy can hide itself in the
most unexpected of places and suddenly reveal itself.

**Prayer: God, we anticipate the joy of celebrating with
others the traditions of our faith and the new year.**

* * * *

LOVE
THE LOVE OF GOD

. . . .

LOVE SENT BY GOD

**Receiving the message of God's love
has the power to change our lives.**

*Verse for the Day: "I pray that you may have the
power to comprehend... what is the breadth and
length and height and depth, and to know the
love... that surpasses knowledge, so that you may be
filled with all the fullness of God"* (Eph 3:18–19).

T OWARD THE END of each episode of the hit TV
series *Touched by an Angel*, Monica announces
to an astonished person that she is an angel sent by
God. More important, she conveys in her gentle Irish
brogue God's message to that person that he loves him
or her.

Week after week, this popular drama portrays human
struggle in many different settings and situations.
Always the crux of the message brought by the angels,
who masquerade as humans, is that God's love is unconditional, and it waits for us to respond to it, to
receive it, and to permit it to transform us.

The message is so simple that it easily escapes our notice and eludes our attention. Sooner or later, however, we experience defining moments—moments when our need for God's love cuts through our cynicism, doubt, and self-sufficiency. It is in these moments that we become willing to seek out the simple but profound offer of divine love. And when we finally do look for it, we find it has been there all along, waiting for us to reach out and take hold of it.

God loves you. Let that truth take hold of you today.

Prayer: As your love, O God, is extended to me today, I receive it gladly.

. . . .

DEMONSTRATING GOD'S LOVE TO OTHERS

The world is a better place whenever we demonstrate God's love.

Verse for the Day: "Love one another. Just as I have loved you, you also should love one another" (John 13:34).

PERHAPS THERE HAS BEEN no more visible example of God's unconditional love in the twentieth century than that of Agnes Gonxha Bojaxhiu, better known to the world as Mother Teresa. Born in 1910 to

Albanian parents, Agnes wanted to serve God. Her burning desire to love and tend to the poorest of the poor led her to establish the Missionaries of Charity in 1950, an order whose vision it is to serve the most destitute of Calcutta—India's untouchable people.

Never marrying or having a family of her own, Mother Teresa made the needy her family. She reached out to them, literally picking them up out of gutters and garbage heaps, to minister God's love to them. In her quiet way, she made a loud proclamation to the world about the nature of God's love: It is unconditional with no strings attached.

In 1979, she was presented with the Nobel peace prize for her humanitarian work. Eventually bad health forced her to step down as superior general of the Missionaries of Charity at the age of 80, but her love for others continued to flow through her every word and deed. She died at 87 on September 5, 1997, but her legacy echoes as a challenge to all who will hear.

"The fruit of prayer is a deepening of faith," she said in her book, *Words to Love By.* "And the fruit of faith is love." And "the greatest of these is love" (1 Cor 13:13).

Prayer: God, let your unconditional love flow out of my life so that those who do not know your love will come to know of it through me.

*   *   *   *

THE CREATOR'S LOVE

Our Creator loved us before we ever came into existence.

Verse for the Day: "I have loved you with an everlasting love" (Jer 31:3).

THE HUGE PIECE OF MARBLE from which Michelangelo sculpted his masterpiece, David, was a difficult slab of stone with which to work. Prior to his trying his hand at it, other noted sculptors had been commissioned to work with it. However, it wasn't until Michelangelo had collected it from the yard of a cathedral workshop that any real progress was made.

Finally, after more than two years of diligently chipping away at the huge block, Michelangelo completed David. It is said that when asked how he had accomplished it, the artist replied that David had been in the stone all along; he, Michelangelo, had simply let the figure out.

The Hebrew shepherd boy, poet, king, and subject of Michelangelo's sculpture, once wrote in a psalm to his Maker, "It was you who formed my inward parts; you knit me together in my mother's womb. I praise you, for I am fearfully and wonderfully made. Wonderful are your works; that I know very well" (Psa 139:13–14).

A creator's love is like no other. It knows before there is life, for it conceives existence from a heart of deep passion. English author G. K. Chesterton once wrote, "The whole difference between construction and creation is exactly this: that a thing constructed can only be loved after constructed; but a thing created is loved before it exists." So it is with the love of God. We came into existence out of his love, and he never retracts that love as long as we live.

Prayer: Creator God, help me remember that the fact that you have made me is evidence of your great love for me.

, , , ,

THE TIES OF FAMILY LOVE

, , , ,

GIVING GRANDMA A LIFT
Family love carries on
from generation to generation.

Verse for the Day: "Let mutual love continue" (Heb 13:1).

THE IDEA OF DRIVING just didn't appeal to my Grandma, so she never bothered getting her license. As I was growing up, I never thought much about the fact that we often gave Grandma a lift when she needed one. When Grandpa was busy or when we were headed in Grandma's direction, we picked her up and were on our way.

I never heard my parents complain about the arrangement. In fact, we all enjoyed it. Of course, we kids always anticipated the moment Grandma would offer us a breath mint.

Now I have personally become an active participant in the giving-Grandma-a-lift tradition. Each week I swing by Grandma's apartment on my way to worship services and pick her up. Sometimes I arrive early, and we chat while she gets ready. On occasion we even extend our morning into an afternoon get-together for lunch.

It's easy to understand now that it wasn't a sense of obligation—or even the breath mint—that turned our family into an alternate set of wheels for Grandma all those years ago; it was simply love.

Grandma's love for us has never wavered, and her love has fueled our love for her and for each other. Giving Grandma a lift has been and continues to be a generational privilege for me—one that has given me a lift—a lift of love.

Prayer: God, thank you that my love for my family continues on in their lives as they love one another.

❦ ❦ ❦ ❦

WHEN LOVE COMES LATER

Love can blossom where it did not previously exist.

Verse for the Day: "May the Lord make you increase and abound in love for one another" (1 Thes 3:12).

MARTIN LUTHER IS best known as the spark that ignited the Protestant Reformation. When he nailed his 95 theses to the door at Wittenberg and translated the Bible into German, he permanently carved his name in history. Yet few people know about the former monk's love affair with his wife and one-time nun, Katherine.

As the story goes, Luther had insisted he would never marry. However, his resolve weakened significantly when he helped 12 nuns escape from a convent and came face to face with Katherine von Bora. When the 41-year-old bachelor and his bride wed in 1525, they were not what most would call "in love," and yet it became evident in their relationship that they had a deep respect for one another. As time passed, their admiration for one another grew into true love, and their marriage became a model of romance and deep affection. They had six children and nurtured them in their happy home.

Martin once smilingly noted, "In domestic affairs I defer to Katie. Otherwise, I am led by the Holy Ghost." Not allowing public opinion about his marriage to affect his enjoyment of the relationship, he boldly replied, "Let them [other men] laugh. God and the angels are smiling in heaven." And with the highest regard for his wife's strengths and abilities, he honestly wrote, "I am an inferior lord, she the superior; I am Aaron, she is my Moses."

Whatever Katherine had or had not felt for her husband on their wedding day had since blossomed into a garden of love. Upon Martin's death, Katherine mourned, "If I had a principality or an empire and lost it, it would not have been as painful as it is now that the dear Lord God has taken from me this precious and beloved man, and not from me alone, but from the whole world."

Love's surprising potential had been realized in the soil of this couple's commitment to one another's best interest. And perhaps the man we know as the "Father of the Reformation" would consider his best achievement to be that of having known the true love of Katherine.

Prayer: God, I welcome the miracle of your love that can grow in the most surprising of places.

❧ ❧ ❧ ❧

LOVE WE CAN COUNT ON

When the world is unkind, loving family
members are a refuge of love.

*Verse for the Day: "Your daughter-in-law who loves
you . . . is more to you than seven sons . . ."* (Ruth 4:15).

A TRAVELING DRAMATIC COMPANY was particularly
well known for one of its leading actresses,
whose theatrical gifts had critics raving. Unfortunately
while on tour, the acclaimed actress came down with a
severe case of laryngitis and could not perform. Nevertheless, her young understudy prepared excitedly and
arranged for her family members to attend the play, for
the company was currently in a city near her home-
town.

That evening, when the announcement was made to
the audience that the awaited performance would be
without the company's star, the crowd murmured its
frustration. Rather than become discouraged, however,
the understudy was inspired to give the performance of
her life. And yet, at her curtain call, she was met with a
still-sulking audience who begrudged her its applause.

Suddenly, a shrill voice cut through the dead silence.
"Oh, Mommy!" A little girl shouted from a seat near
the back of the theater. "You're the best in the world!"

The crowd turned to see a four year old standing on her chair, her tiny hands raised in adulation as she fiercely clapped for her mother. The child's overture of love melted the hearts of the disgruntled theater-goers, and at once they offered a round of well-deserved applause to the teary-eyed understudy.

Strangers can be unkind, unbending, and unappreciative of what we have to offer. Sometimes we limp away from our encounters with others, badly wounded and needing a place to heal. Fortunately, those who enjoy the blessing of strong family ties can find the healing they need in the protective environment of family relationships.

When we feel defeated by the outside world, we can remember that our families know and love us best. They see us, really see us. And there is, perhaps, no one else in the world more qualified than a loving family member to say, "I think you are wonderful!"

Prayer: God, thank you that my family, whether made up of relatives or otherwise, is a refuge for my soul.

* * * *

THE SPECIAL LOVE OF FRIENDS

. . . .

A FRIEND FOR A LIFETIME

The rare kind of friendship that lasts a lifetime is one that becomes a special part of us.

Verse for the Day: "Some friends play at friendship but a true friend sticks closer than one's nearest kin" (Prov 18:24).

O NE OF MODERN HISTORY'S most admired women is Helen Keller, who became a renowned lecturer worldwide though she had neither eyesight nor hearing. Yet Helen Keller did not overcome her personal obstacles and arrive at success on her own. She had a friend, who became very much a part of who she was.

As a child, Helen was introduced to Anne Sullivan, a young woman who had been orphaned at an early age. Half blind and penniless when her mother passed away, Anne was sent to a local poor house. Later, however, at the Perkins Institute for the Blind, a skilled physician performed an operation that restored her sight. Not surprisingly, Anne Sullivan's passion turned toward caring for and teaching others who were blind.

When Anne was asked to work with Helen Keller, the teacher soon discovered that her pupil was exceptionally bright. Anne's innovation and skill in guiding her pupil, combined with Helen's sharp mind, produced incredible results. In just a couple of weeks, Helen knew 30 words. From those early lessons, Helen continued to learn and grow as a person. For 49 years, student and teacher were inseparable friends.

During that time, Anne faced her own great obstacle when she lost her sight once again. During this ordeal, it was Helen who helped Anne adjust to the world of blindness. They remained devoted friends until Anne's death in 1936.

A friend for a lifetime, a kindred spirit. If we have been blessed with such a relationship, we likely understand what a rare gift we have been given. In the Bible, David and Jonathan were companions whose friendship could not be broken by anything but death although it was severely tested by adversity. When his friend fell in war, David lamented that the depth of his love for Jonathan had surpassed that of any relationship he had ever known.

Rare and wonderful are friendships that fill our souls as to become a part of who we are. They never leave us—never. And we hold them in our hearts for eternity.

Prayer: God, I thank you for the rare privilege of an eternal friendship with you.

❄ ❄ ❄ ❄

THE BLESSING OF BEST FRIENDS

The deepest relationships we share are often with best friends.

Verse for the Day: "Greatly beloved were you to me; your love to me was wonderful" (2 Sam 1:26).

M Y FIRST BEST FRIEND was Christina. We met in kindergarten and were virtually inseparable through the fourth grade.

We shared adventures: going to the swamp behind her house to hunt for treasure. We shared trouble: getting a lecture after the chocolate chips we had hidden in her room were discovered by her basset hound and subsequently chewed and drooled all over the carpet. We shared secrets: letting each other read our lock-and-key diaries. We shared pain: saying goodbye when I transferred to another school in the fifth grade.

While moving to a new residence, I recently came across a small book given to me by Christina, entitled *Close to You, That's Where I'd Like to Be.* It features cute pictures of cats and kittens that are captioned with expressions of friendship. The front of the book was signed by Christina and given to me in 1974. What has kept me from getting rid of that silly little book? Simply the memory of my relationship with my first best friend. It remains a blessing in my life.

What best friends have blessed your life with their trust and love? Have you told the best friend in your life right now the things you love best about him or her? It's good to say the mushy stuff sometimes, even if your friend isn't transferring to another school.

Prayer: When I think of my best friends, dear God, it warms my spirit to know how well they love me.

*   *   *   *

BEFRIENDING THE FRIENDLESS

Extending friendship to others is a beautiful gift of love.

Verse for the Day: "All who saw it began to grumble and said, "[Jesus] has gone to be the guest of one who is a sinner" (Luke 19:7).

AS PRESIDENT, ABRAHAM LINCOLN received a constant flow of correspondence from soldiers seeking pardon and relief from the military's code of discipline. These appeals generally were accompanied with letters of support from influential friends. On one occasion, however, an unusual letter crossed the president's desk. It was a one-page request for pardon. There were no enclosures, no signatures from notable people, no endorsements.

"What! Has this man no friends?" asked the president.

"No, sir, not one," the staff officer confirmed.

"Then, I will be his friend," Lincoln declared and at once granted the soldier's request.

Friendship is a powerful element in our lives. The presence of a friend assures us that we're not alone—that there's someone in our corner rooting for us. If we've ever felt friendless and then had someone come alongside us, offering their support, comfort, and love, we know how meaningful the gift of friendship can be. In times of loneliness, trouble, and uncertainty, we long for our friends. And when we see others struggling alone, we can choose to be a friend to them—to be for them what others have been for us. In doing so, we pass along one of the most coveted of love's gifts—the gift of friendship.

Prayer: God, you have extended friendship to me without condition; it is because of your love that I can reach out to someone in need of friendship today.

* * * *

THE GIFT OF PETS

. . . .

CONSOLED BY CRITTERS

Our pets are a source of comfort and consolation.

Verse for the Day: "The poor man had ... one little ewe lamb, which he had bought. He brought it up, and it grew up with him and with his children; it used to eat of his meager fare, and drink from his cup, and lie in his bosom, and it was like a daughter to him" (2 Sam 12:3).

*A*NYONE WHO'S EVER KNOWN what it is to have a favorite pet knows the consolation a critter can be. Muffin, a longhair, female cat, happened to be the critter in my life during my teen years—those years many of us would sooner forget.

At that time, Muffin was everything I could have wanted in a friend. If I needed to verbalize a problem or struggle, she would lie at the foot of my bed as I paced the room and recited my frustration to her— her attentive gaze following me back and forth. If for some reason I silently cried at night, she would lick my face and purr loudly, comforting me. When I had a secret, I could tell her without fear of an information leak. When I just needed to sit quietly and think, she would curl up in my lap and sleep, keeping me company without disturbing my solitude. She had no advice to give and no judgments to pass. When I needed to feel unconditionally accepted, Muffin was the friend I could always turn to.

Various cats, dogs, hamsters, fish, birds, and even frogs have seen me through various phases of my childhood and adult years (some of these, of course, providing more camaraderie than others). Yet each of them has been a gift—another living presence to tend and watch and talk to. Each has been a consolation to me in its own way from time to time.

What critters have been or continue to be a part of your experience? Consider the comfort and warm consolation they've provided. It's no accident that you have enjoyed their company and known their love. Certainly our common Maker—Creator of animals and humans—intended it to be that way. Such relationships between people and beasts are yet another special gift to us from God's imaginative mind and tender heart.

Prayer: My pets, Creator, have been to me a source of comfort and consolation—a cherished gift from your hand.

❧ ❧ ❧ ❧

LIFE PRINCIPLES FROM OUR LOVING PETS

Positive character qualities in pets can inspire us to be better people.

Verse for the Day: "But ask the animals, and they will teach you" (Job 12:7).

*A*NIMALS, AS WE OBSERVE THEIR WAYS, sometimes have a lesson or two to pass along to the human race. By their wordless example, they convey to us useful tidbits of wisdom about life and love.

Here are some insights about our pets from which we can learn: Always greet those you love with affection and exuberance; if someone gets after you for blowing it, do your best to apologize, make up, and move on; when there's danger, sound an alert; be friendly, loyal, courageous, transparent, and forgiving; be easygoing while playing with children; if you're happy, wear a smile; find a warm spot in the sunshine and soak in it; pursue your goals with intensity; enjoy the great outdoors as much as possible; if you want attention, ask for it in a straightforward manner; when someone offers you a treat, don't be too proud to come running to get it; establish good relationships with your neighbors; and take each new day as it comes.

Many of us can relate experiences when our pet has sensed our mood during moments of sadness and has come to comfort us. Some of us can relate inspiring stories of our pet's loyalty and courage. Nearly all pet owners can relate to the unconditional affection their pet has demonstrated toward them. Of course, pets don't always behave as we want them to. They have their quirks, mishaps, and stubborn streaks. In their better moments, however, they remind us of some of life's important principles and simple pleasures.

Prayer: God, thank you for the ways my pets have enhanced my love and enjoyment of life.

✹　✹　✹　✹

PEACE

PEACE THAT COMES FROM FAITH

• • • •

FAITH FOR THE FUTURE

Being able to trust the future to God gives us a great deal of peace.

Verse for the Day: "We know that all things work together for good for those who love God, who are called according to his purpose" (Rom 8:28).

PSYCHICS COMMONLY APPEAR on television commercials these days, offering potential customers the benefit of their powers of clairvoyance. Part of the advertisements include the testimonials of people who claim to have been helped by psychic services. These individuals tell how accurate the assessments they received were. Some even shed tears. As a result, new customers call in, seeking answers and wanting to know what the future might hold for them.

What makes people so desperate to know the future? Why do they resort to consulting Ouija boards, fortune tellers, psychics, and palm readers? The answer is readily found in our own frustrations with uncertainty. The unknown is simply unbearable at times. We cannot see what's ahead, and we feel we must know or go crazy. While God asks us to trust him, we may hesitate to take the next step, because what if...?

What we might sometimes lose sight of, and what people phoning the psychic hotlines don't realize, is that finding out the future does not put us any closer to being able to successfully meet it. If we were uncertain about the future to begin with, we still cannot be sure that the advice of a fortune teller is going to come true anyway. We are right back in the same uncertainty we faced in the first place.

As people of faith, however, we have every advantage for welcoming the future, no matter what it may hold. There is no need to know what lies ahead, for we already know that God is there to walk with us through it. Knowing all of the details would actually spoil our journey. The good stuff would fail to be pleasantly surprising, and the difficulties would cause us needless worry. As it is, we can trust that we will come against no insurmountable obstacles with the Lord as our guide. In that assurance, there is unparalleled inner peace.

Prayer: God of the past, present, and future, I am your child, and my future rests securely in your care.

❧ ❧ ❧ ❧

Peaceful Confidence in God

When we trust God, we are less fearful to take action in the face of danger.

Verse for the Day: "The peace of God, which surpasses all understanding, will guard your hearts and your minds in Christ Jesus" (Phlp 4:7).

THE GREAT MISSIONARY Hudson Taylor believed in expressing trust in God through prayer. On his first trip to China aboard a sailing ship, the wind had died down and a four-knot current was carrying the ship ever closer to a sunken reef just off the coast of New Guinea.

The captain, of course, was concerned. It was only a matter of time before his ship would be torn apart on the reef. When Taylor spoke to the captain and learned of the predicament, Taylor suggested that the four men of faith on board, which included the captain, spend some time in prayer, asking God for wind.

The captain readily agreed, and all four men retired to their cabins to present their need to God. After a brief time of prayer, Taylor came out on deck and asked the first officer to let down the mainsail. Reluctant to comply, the first officer asked what good it would do to let it down in the absence of wind.

Taylor explained that wind was coming, that he and the others had asked as much of God. Not impressed by Taylor's logic, the first officer said that he'd much rather see some wind than just hear about it.

Just then, as the ship was about to make contact with the reef, a breeze stirred in the topmost sail. Taylor urged the first officer to let down the mainsail; there was no time to lose. Still unconvinced, but having nothing to lose, the annoyed officer dropped the mainsail with an air of contempt. At once the huge sail mushroomed, and the wind that had suddenly filled the sails carried the ship well past the islands and out of danger.

Hudson Taylor had an abiding confidence in God. So certain was he in God's ability to send wind that his first response to danger was prayer, revealing a deep and peaceful trust that would characterize his life of service.

Prayer: God, may my actions reveal a peaceful trust in your goodness.

❦ ❦ ❦ ❦

Peace in God's Limitlessness

Peace comes in being confident that God's resources are limitless.

Verse for the Day: "The heavens are yours, the earth also is yours; the world and all that is in it—you have founded them" (Psa 89:11).

*H*AROLD AND JOAN had determined that each time one of their grandchildren turned 12 years old, they would take that child on the vacation of his or her choice. Melissa was Harold and Joan's oldest grandchild, and upon turning 12, she chose Florida as her destination.

In the course of planning the event, Melissa became concerned. "This is going to take a lot of money, Grandma," she noted. "Can you afford this?"

As the oldest child in her family, Melissa had come to understand the limitations of a family budget. What she didn't understand, however, is that her grandparents were not limited in the same sense as her parents were. Joan and Harold, much further down the road of life than their son and daughter-in-law, were reaping the benefits of years of financial planning.

It was difficult for Melissa to fathom that finances were not a concern on this outing. Nevertheless, after much reassuring, she began to relax and trust that she was in no danger of breaking the bank by requesting many of the things she wanted to do in Florida.

Similarly, at times, we may project human limitations on God—limitations he simply does not have. "Can you afford this?" we may question, wondering if maybe we've asked for too much from him.

"Afford it?" the Lord may well smile. "It belongs to me. Trust me that I'll do what's very best for you as you walk with me."

It may take reassuring from God's Word and from others for us to become convinced that God's resources are limitless, but once it begins to sink in, our worry will melt away as faith replaces anxiety and peace prevails in our hearts.

Prayer: Let the knowledge of your limitlessness fill my heart with peace, dear God.

* * * *

PEACE THAT COMES WITH MATURITY

. . . .

PEACE IN TRUSTING GOD'S PROVIDENCE

As we mature, we find peace of mind in trusting that God has our best interest at heart.

Verse for the Day: "A tranquil mind gives life to the flesh" (Prov 14:30).

RICHARD HALVERSON, former Senate chaplain, once said he believed God knows us so well that his care for us includes just the right amounts of happiness and sadness. He knows just how much material blessings to give us and how much to withhold. He permits just the right amount of adversity and gives exactly enough peace so we will grow up to be strong and wise.

In youth, a fighting spirit might be beneficial for starting out in life and making one's way in a challenging world. At times, however, that fighting spirit may mistakenly strive against what God intends for one's good. For example, God may permit financial struggle to draw a child of his toward a deeper understanding of his ability to provide. Yet with an immature perspective and the natural instinct to fight against adversity, one may take time to discover God's loving intentions.

In contrast, as life's experiences mature us, we will realize that God's blessings, as well as the trials he permits, are all part of the care with which he intimately tends our lives. As we learn to trust his providence, the anxious struggling against adversity gives way to a peace of mind that knows there is a good purpose and plan behind each dark night and each bright day.

Prayer: God, my mind has learned to be at peace in every situation, as I have come to trust in your loving care.

* * * *

THE PEACE OF PATIENCE
Life's waiting stages teach us the peaceful art of patience.

~(B)~

Verse for the Day: "Indeed we call blessed those who showed endurance. You have heard of the endurance of Job, and you have seen the purpose of the Lord, how the Lord is compassionate and merciful" (Jas 5:11).

IN LIFE WE MUST WAIT for many things. As small children, we wait until we're old enough to go to school and do things older children are doing, such as riding a bicycle and climbing a tree. Young teens wait restlessly until they can finally get their driver's license and the freedom that comes with having access to a car. College students and apprentices put in time and study as they anticipate a career in their chosen field. And once in their vocations, workers strive and wait for promotions and raises. Young couples save money, waiting for the day when they can afford to buy their first home. Middle adults look forward to retirement, and so on.

After so much waiting in life, we either become entirely frustrated or we grow increasingly patient. Of course, the latter is more desirable. There is something about the patient person that can bring calm to a group. And it's usually the older, mature person who fills the role of calming the often rash notions of youth.

Reflect a little on your own journey toward gaining a patient spirit. What things have you waited for in life? What experiences have contributed most to your learn-ing the peaceful art of patience? You might be surprised to discover that your calming ways have been born out of a good number of simple, but not-so-easy, waiting experiences. Indeed, it's this mature patience that pro-vides peace and stability not only to your life but also to those around you.

Prayer: God, though waiting hasn't been easy, you've taught me to be patient and peaceful and to trust in your timing.

❧ ❧ ❧ ❧

THE PEACEFUL FRUIT OF INSIGHT

There is a peace that comes
with the insights of maturity.

*Verse for the Day: "Lay aside immaturity,
and live, and walk in the way of insight"* (Prov 9:6).

A RUSSIAN WRITER named Panin once said that he
considered three kinds of individuals to be his
friends: First, those who love him; second, those who
hate him; and third, those who are indifferent toward
him. Why? Panin explained that the loving people in
his life helped him learn sensitivity; the hateful people
helped him learn to be careful; and the indifferent
people helped him learn to be more self-disciplined.
Panin had found friends, in a manner of speaking, even
in his enemies, for he understood that there was something to be gained from each of life's situations and in
each human encounter.

Such insight can come only from a mature mind, from
one who not only has experience but has also looked
for and found the benefit of that experience. And what
is the benefit of this positive insight? The benefit is
peace.

In his mind, Panin was at peace with everyone. He could see how each of them, even by a negative experience, could have a positive effect on his life when he chose to see it that way. We, too, can be at peace in each of life's situations as we apply our insight and find the deeper meanings and greater possibilities of our experiences.

Prayer: God, grant me the insight to see the positive purposes you have for me in each day and fill me with the peace that comes from living by that insight.

* * * *

THE PEACE OF A GENTLE SPIRIT
Our gentle ways are a peaceful refuge for tired souls.

Verse for the Day: "Let your gentleness be known to everyone" (Phlp 4:5).

BEFORE DANIEL WEBSTER BECAME a great statesman and orator, his ambition to study law brought him to Boston, where he worked in the office of Christopher Gore, who headed the Massachusetts bar. Because Webster had not followed protocol and had entered the office uninvited, the young law student found himself being treated as an outsider—generally ignored and looked upon with contempt.

One day, however, politician Rufus King came into the office and noticed that Webster was all by himself. Understanding the situation, King made a point of going over to the lonely student, shaking his hand, and engaging him in warm conversation. "I know your father well," King said. "Be studious and you will win. If you need any assistance or advice, come to me." Much later in his life, when Webster had become famous, he recalled the brief exchange with King and said, "I can still feel the warm pressure of that hand, and hear those challenging words of encourgement."

Our gentleness speaks peace to those who are worn out from conflict. The battles they face may be from without or within. Yet our gentle spirit can be a place of refuge for them, a shelter where they can rest awhile and gain strength to continue pressing on.

Take a moment to be a gentle presence, speak a gentle word, and give a gentle touch to someone who seems worn down today. In that moment of gentleness, you will transfer a bit of peace and rest into their souls from which they can gather strength.

Prayer: As your gentleness gives me peace and rest, God, so let my gentleness impart peace to others today.

❦ ❦ ❦ ❦

A Peaceful Spirit Among Others

* * * *

Handel, a Peacemaker

For us to pursue peace is at the heart of God's desires for humankind.

Verse for the Day: "Glory to God in the highest heaven, and on earth peace among those whom he favors!" (Luke 2:14).

SINCE ITS FIRST PERFORMANCE IN 1742, the stirring strains of Handel's *Messiah* have deeply moved audiences throughout the world. Amazingly, the entire composition took only 24 days to complete. Few people know, however, that the music was written for a benefit to raise money for an orphan's hospital. Handel loved people and always sought, not only to give generously, but also to promote peace and goodwill.

The composer George Frideric Handel was born in Halle, Germany, on February 23, 1685. Handel's father, also named George, held a position in the royal court as a surgeon. The elder George's hopes for his son included the study of law; young George's passion, however, was for music, and while accompanying his father on trips to court, the boy taught himself to play the instruments he came across while at the palace.

One day the boy's prodigious talent impressed the duke, who persuaded Handel's father to let his son take formal lessons. As Handel studied with the organist at a local church, he quickly became accomplished and played regularly for services. As early as age 18, Handel's reputation as a composer was well known.

Unfortunately, Handel's success stirred envy in others who set out to make his life miserable. Despite spiteful actions toward him, such as orchestras being purposely scheduled to perform at the same time Handel had chosen for his concerts, the great composer did not seek revenge. Financial ruin threatened, and his health gave out from time to time under the intense pressure he experienced, but he never resorted to using his influence to get even with his persecutors.

Sadly, some of his harshest critics came from within the church. The fact that he was performing his God-honoring music in regular concert halls, rather than in the church, provoked preachers to indignation. He became the target of fiery sermons. Yet he responded by holding his tongue and bearing no malice. He was committed to living out the Bible's mandate to forgive, and even at great personal cost, he sought peace with those who tried to tear him apart.

Although unquestionably one of the greatest composers of all time, George Frideric Handel was also a man of great character, whose desire for peace—even peace with his enemies—was always paramount to personal gain.

Prayer: God of peace, grant me a spirit of peace that I can extend to others.

FROM FEAR TO FUN

Our reassuring presence and words can transfer peace to children.

Verse for the Day: "In . . . the Lord one has strong confidence, and one's children will have refuge" (Prov 14:26).

JOSHUA WAS TAKING CARE of his two young grandchildren one evening when the house suddenly became dark. A downed power line had knocked out the electricity in the neighborhood. Terrified of the sudden pitch dark, the grandchildren began to wail. While he assured them that it would be OK, Joshua quickly located a flashlight and then sat down to hold the children in his arms until they became calm again.

Next, Grandpa Josh went to work spinning his magic. He brought out candles and kerosene lamps, which filled the house with a soft glow. He lit a fire in the fireplace and helped the children toast marshmallows, as together the threesome pretended they were on a camping trip. This loving grandpa had turned a frightening experience into a perfect adventure.

When the lights came back on, the children groaned in disappointment. "We're having fun!" they cried.

By our peaceful spirit, we have the power to transfer calm to children who may be looking anxiously about them for reassurance. Though their lives may be full of turmoil, we can be a presence that instills a measure of much-needed confidence and tranquility. When we speak to them, our steadiness becomes their own as they borrow strength from our deep reservoir of peace.

Prayer: God, allow my peace to become a resting place for those who need its comfort.

⚜ ⚜ ⚜ ⚜

WHAT'S YOUR SECRET?
When we have a peaceful spirit, others want to know our secret.

Verse for the Day: "I will both lie down and sleep in peace; for you alone, O Lord, make me lie down in safety" (Psa 4:8).

WHEN EMPEROR AUGUSTUS OF ROME learned that a certain man slept peaceably each night though he owed a large sum of money to his debtors, the emperor became determined to acquire the man's bed. After striking the deal, however, and then trying out his new acquisition, the emperor found that he had made a futile purchase. Not surprisingly, the bed made no difference in his ability to get a good night's sleep.

So if it wasn't the bed, what was the gentleman of Rome's secret? Perhaps it was the same as King David's, which is really no secret at all. David found it easy to sleep peacefully—even when people wanted to kill him—because he believed wholeheartedly that God was taking care of him.

When our trust is in God's providence, our spirit is at peace. And when peace pervades our lives, people who find such rest elusive will want to know our secret. Is it our exercise routine? Our diet? Special vitamins? Our circumstances? Our disposition? Our bank account?

They may be surprised when we say, "None of the above." It's possible that they may not believe us when we reveal the truth, but we can tell them anyway. A little verse in the Book of Isaiah sums it up quite well: "Those of steadfast mind [Lord God] you keep in peace—in peace because they trust in you" (Isa 26:3).

Prayer: God, knowing you are in control of my life is the secret of my peace. Thank you.

* * * *

THE POWER OF PEACEFUL LEADERSHIP

Peaceful leadership has the power to bring about lasting change in others.

Verse for the Day: "Let us then pursue what makes for peace and for mutual upbuilding" (Rom 14:19).

AS AN AFRICAN AMERICAN MAN who had grown up in a pre-civil-rights South, Dr. Martin Luther King, Jr., had seen and experienced his share of prejudice, injustice, and hatred. As he pursued his education, his mind and social consciousness were sharpened, and his passion for social issues grew. Dr. King struggled, however, to know how to approach the evils he saw against his people and the poor in general.

While King wrestled with these issues, he became impressed by the life and teachings of Mahatma Gandhi, the Indian leader whose doctrine of nonviolent civil disobedience struck a chord with King. As a result, King embraced the philosophy of Gandhi's nonviolent leadership through peaceful protest and began to employ it as the means of making his message heard.

Peacefully and eloquently, King decried social injustice, waking the moral and social consciousness of a nation that had long been in a deep slumber of ignorance and indifference. With his vibrant voice, he shouted the truth, and by his actions, he rejected falsehood. Like a wrecking ball, the truth, peacefully presented, did what no amount of violence could have accomplished. The once impenetrable walls of injustice began to crumble.

In 1964, due largely to the leadership of Dr. King, the Civil Rights Bill was passed. That same year, Dr. Martin Luther King, Jr., became the youngest person ever to receive the Nobel peace prize. As a result, *Time* magazine featured him as "Man of the Year," the first African American ever to receive that honor.

It is evident in his writings, speeches, and sermons that King believed in the power and truth of God's word. In 1963, King preached a sermon entitled "Tough Mind—Tender Heart." In it, he encouraged his congregation to recall the words of Jesus, who said, "Be ye therefore wise as serpents, and harmless as doves" (Matt 10:16).

Dr. Martin Luther King, Jr., lived out this command of Christ in the social arena. He was not only a leader who demonstrated wisdom but also one who was committed to peace. As people of faith, we, too, must be people who lead with the power of our peaceful ways.

Prayer: God, you have shown us the way of peaceful leadership; unleash the power of that peace in my life as well.

* * * *

PERSONAL GROWTH

SEEKING NEW EXPERIENCES

. . . .

LIFE BEGINS AT 80!

Many exciting experiences become more accessible to us as we get older.

Verse for the Day: "Those who wait for the Lord shall renew their strength, they shall mount up with wings like eagles, they shall run and not be weary, they shall walk and not faint" (Isa 40:31).

IT'S BEEN SAID life begins at 80. That's good news, because it seems as if the previous years consist of an awful lot of struggling just to get by. The story of an 84-year-old woman gives us reason to hope and believe that life in one's eighties can truly be exciting.

Marion Rice Hart was called "The Flying Grandmother." When she was 84, she piloted an airplane across the Atlantic. In fact, she flew her single-engine plane solo from Washington, D.C., to Iceland, England, France, Italy, and Greece. Truly, age is irrelevant when it comes to striking out on new adventures.

Recently a woman in her seventies inspired me when I was vacationing in Maui. This vibrant woman was on the same snorkeling excursion I was on. Chatting with her as we both waited our turn to get off the boat and into the water, I discovered that she was on the trip by herself and had never snorkeled before in her life. I had to admire her courage and sense of adventure.

As a first-time snorkeler myself, I was definitely nervous, but I was with friends without whom I would not have signed up! While I fancy myself as a bit of an adventurer, this woman had me beat, hands down.

Prayer: God, thank you for these years of being able to take hold of new and wonderful experiences.

* * * *

I'VE-ALWAYS-WANTED-TO-DO LIST
It's never too late to take action on your list of things you'd like to do.

Verse for the Day: "Commit your work to the Lord, and your plans will be established" (Prov 16:3).

WHAT'S ON YOUR I've-always-wanted-to-do list? A trip? A college course? Playing an instrument? Pilot lessons?

Ingrid had always wanted to visit the Holy Land, but somehow after 60-plus years she'd just never gotten around to looking into it. There was always something in the way—the expense would be too great, the timing was not good, or there were other more pressing considerations. Finally, Ingrid realized there would never be a good time to make the trip. So she took the plunge, made the travel arrangements, and had the time of her life.

It has been said that it's doubtful if anyone ever made an attempt at anything who waited until all the conditions were just right before starting. Allowing circumstances to be the deciding factor in one's course of action leaves no opportunity for purposeful living. English playwright George Bernard Shaw said that the people who make the most of life are those who search for the right moments and opportunities for accomplishing their dreams and goals, but if those circumstances aren't at hand, such people know how to find a way to make their dreams happen anyway.

Of course, to live purposefully is not to abandon consideration of our circumstances or of other people in our lives. Yet those people who have a purpose and who acknowledge obstacles do not permit surmountable obstacles to deter them from realizing their goals and living out their dreams.

Take a look at your I've-always-wanted-to-do list and write down what obstacles are in the way of your doing that thing beside each item. Survey those problems and think of ways you can overcome them. Finally, determine to live purposefully by making plans to shorten your list by realizing one or more of your dreams.

Prayer: God, as I prayerfully plan my course of action, I trust in you to guide my steps.

* * *

HAVING AN ADVENTUROUS SPIRIT

An adventurous spirit welcomes new experiences.

Verse for the Day: "God did not give us a spirit of cowardice, but rather a spirit of power and of love and of self-discipline" (2 Tim 1:7).

SEVERAL YEARS AGO, travel agencies in Brussels struck upon a marketing idea that turned out to be highly successful. They began selling "Mystery Tours" to adventurous tourists who wanted to go on a trip in which they had no idea where they'd be going.

New experiences bring with them many question marks: What about...? What if...? Will I...? Though a thousand such questions arise, an adventurous spirit moves eagerly forward to greet the answers.

John, an adventurer at heart, never passes up an opportunity to meet new people or go to new places. So when the social club for seniors to which he belonged was electing an event planner, John's name naturally came up, and he was a shoo-in for the position.

As event coordinator, John always delights his peers with interesting day trips and weekend getaways in picturesque settings, but his favorite event of all is the annual "mystery trip." From his vast collection of brochures of places to go and things to do, John begins to formulate his plan. Careful to keep the destination a secret, he covertly arranges the details. His goal is always to provide an experience that includes unique and enjoyable activities. One time, the mystery-trip's bus pulled into a dude ranch, where everyone could take carriage rides, pan for gold, eat a chuck-wagon-style meal, and listen (or dance) to authentic hoedown music.

"Being adventurous keeps me young at heart," John says. And with his knack for finding new places to see and new things to do, he helps others stay that way, too.

Prayer: God, grant me a continual spirit of adventure to enjoy each new experience you bring.

* * * *

EMBRACING NEW CHALLENGES

, , , ,

MISSION POSSIBLE

**Many more things are possible
than we imagine when we
determine to meet life's challenges.**

*Verse for the Day: "But you, take courage!
Do not let your hands be weak, for your work
shall be rewarded" (2 Chron 15:7).*

WHEN THE GREAT auto manufacturer, Henry Ford, sought to develop safety glass for his cars, he consulted his engineers. All but one of the 130 said there were too many reasons why the idea wouldn't work. That one visionary engineer believed it could be accomplished despite the many obstacles. He set to work and developed safety glass. Perhaps this was one of the many experiences in Henry Ford's life that prompted him to believe that people are capable of doing more than they think they can do.

Have you been handed a seemingly impossible challenge? While it's true that there are some things that are impossible for us, there are many others that, though difficult, are attainable. Ponder Henry Ford's confidence in people and then determine to give your best effort to each challenge you meet.

Although we may need to step back from a challenge at times and take a rest from it, it's important that we don't give up until we have given it our best shot. As long as there are still more possibilities to explore, more angles to examine, and more energy to give, we can keep trying. And quite often mission impossible becomes mission possible as a result of our tenacity.

Prayer: God, all things are possible for you, and with you in my life many more things are possible for me when I trust you to bless my best efforts to meet life's challenges.

* * * *

BUILDING THE BROOKLYN BRIDGE

When a new challenge becomes a passion, there is no limit to what we can do.

Verse for the Day: "Be strong in the Lord and in the strength of his power" (Eph 6:10).

THE PROSPECT OF BUILDING a 1,600-foot-long, single-span suspension bridge that would reach from Manhattan to Brooklyn seemed impossible to most people. Yet an enterprising engineer named John

Roebling believed it could be done and he was the man who could do it. His son, Washington, was also an engineer who became convinced of the plausibility of his father's plan. Together they undertook to secure approval and finances for building their dream bridge.

Opponents to the idea, however, were not so easily persuaded. Ferryboat operators protested loudly, because a bridge would threaten their livelihood. Other engineers were sure it was just too large a feat. At the same time, plans for a tunnel were vying for acceptance. It took six long years of financial, political, and technical debate, but finally in 1869, the Roeblings were able to begin work on their bridge.

Soon after the project was underway, John was surveying the location for one of the bridge's towers from a pier. One of the loose pilings somehow crushed his foot, and he died of tetanus shortly afterward. This was a tragic blow for Washington, but his mission to complete his father's brilliant plan was not defeated. He continued to work on the site day after day.

Unfortunately, Washington, along with many of the workers who labored in the underwater chambers while the tower's foundations were laid, suffered from "caisson disease" or the bends. In 1872, Washington became so crippled by it that he was confined to his bed, paralyzed and unable to talk.

Determined to finish the task, however, he lay in his bed, where he could look through field glasses and see the work in progress from a window. Thus he relayed plans to the workers through his wife, Emily, who would take her husband's instructions to the site.

On May 24, 1883, 14 years after it was started, Washington Roebling watched from the window of his townhome as the city of New York celebrated the opening of the magnificent Brooklyn Bridge—then the longest suspension bridge in the world.

Prayer: While I face the new challenges in my life, God, grant me the strength to meet and master them.

*   *   *   *

JUMP AS HIGH AS YOU CAN
Getting rid of false limitations
frees us to meet new challenges.

~⟨♡⟩~

Verse for the Day: "I can do all things through him who strengthens me" (Phlp 4:13).

DID YOU KNOW THAT FLEAS are trainable? You've heard the saying: You say, "Jump," and I'll ask, "How high?" Well, flea trainers have developed a technique for teaching their pupils just how high to jump. Rookie fleas are placed in a box of a determined height. The lid is placed on the box. The trainees jump hard at first, knocking their heads on the top of the box. But eventually they jump only as high as they can without bumping into the lid. Interestingly, even after being let out of the box, they'll not attempt to jump any higher.

It reminds me of something about human nature. Sometimes we get placed—by ourselves or by others—into "boxes" of limitation. These limitations may be a result of fear, failure, or any number of negative influences in our lives. It is often from within those confines of what we believe about our ability that we stop short of what we are truly capable. Because of the false sense of ineptness, we refuse to accept challenges that will stretch us to new levels of accomplishment.

After a flea is trained, it forgets the time when it could jump much higher. Perhaps there was a time when we believed we could climb much higher, go much further, and be much more. What if we could return to that sort of faith? What if we could put behind us painful memories that have deterred us from rising to meet new challenges? What if we decided to jump as hard as we could at the next challenge that presented itself? We would, no doubt, end up jumping right out of the box, moving on quickly to new and wonderful horizons.

Prayer: God, I seek your help to free me from false limitations so I can reach the full potential you've put within me.

❧ ❧ ❧ ❧

DEVELOPING NEW STRENGTHS

* * * *

TURNING WEAKNESS INTO STRENGTH

Our steady, consistent efforts will succeed in turning weaknesses into strengths.

Verse for the Day: "Lift your drooping hands and strengthen your weak knees" (Heb 12:12).

IT WAS DAMP, CHILLY, AND RAINY outside this morning while I donned my exercise clothes. Ugh! What an awful day for a run! But I had promised myself that I would get out at least three times this week in an effort to begin getting back in shape. Here it was Saturday morning, and I had been out only twice—once on Tuesday and once on Thursday. It was either go out now or break my promise. So I went.

The tough part about turning any weakness into a strength—whether it's a strength we lost somewhere along the way, or it's a brand-new strength we want to acquire—is that at first it seems as if our efforts are doing little or nothing to get us to where we'd like to be. As I've huffed and puffed up and down the sidewalks and streets this week, I've been able to go a mere fraction of the distance I used to run. It takes a lot more effort than it used to. To add insult to injury, the stingy old scale hasn't budged even half a pound!

Of course, I know, as you know, that people who run marathons don't just wake up one morning out of the blue and decide they're going to run the big race in Boston. Nor do weight lifters just wander off the street into the gym and press several hundred pounds of steel over their head with no prior training.

No, strengthening is a process. It demands a combination of our desire, our will power, our commitment, and our patience. There are no shortcuts, secrets, or miracle methods to build strength in any area of life, whether physical, mental, emotional, or spiritual. The formula is plain and simple: Steady consistent effort gets results. In fact, part of the joy of reaching such goals lies in knowing that there was difficulty, struggle, even setbacks on the path to achievement, and we persisted and overcame them all.

Therefore, it helps a great deal to know that in developing a new strength our daily efforts are small but significant victories along the way to the big, end-result celebration. Allow the little wins to encourage you; don't let them escape your notice. We need them as cheerleaders along the way to help us keep going.

What weakness are you wanting to or working to turn into a strength right now? May I suggest that you not look at how far you have to go? Just determine that today you'll take the next step on the path to getting there. And as you take this step and the next and the next, the strength you seek will become yours along the way.

Prayer: God, grant me desire, willpower, commitment, and patience along this path to becoming strong.

* * * *

BECOMING STRONGER
As we allow God to nurture us with his own strength, we become stronger.

Verse for the Day: "Happy are those whose strength is in you, ... They go from strength to strength" (Psa 84:5, 7).

LUTHER BURBANK WAS a late nineteenth-early twentieth-century American horticulturist. He created hundreds of new varieties of fruits, vegetables, and flowers. Without the aid of any scientific theory, he taught himself the complicated techniques of plant crossing, selection, and hybridization.

For a half century, Burbank tended his garden, meandering among his beloved plants. Today we enjoy the results of his work: thornless blackberries; larger, tastier potatoes; plums that have no pits; walnuts that open more easily, and so much more.

As a watchful caretaker, Burbank had a special gift for coaxing his garden to disclose its secrets to him. He saw each flower, each tree, each plant, as having special potential. He learned from each its unique characteristics, strengths, and weaknesses, and then he would teach each one how to become greater— more beautiful, more fragrant, more fruitful, or more useful.

Luther Burbank tended his plants with the strength of his knowledge, and as a result, they became more wonderful than ever. Similarly, as we allow God, the all-knowing Gardener of our souls, to nurture our lives with his own strength, we ourselves become better people, are able to love and serve more effectively, and achieve greatness in his kingdom.

Prayer: God, you are the caretaker of human souls, and only you can make us strong as we serve you.

*   *   *   *

Exploring New Ideas

. . . .

Asking "What If?"

Creative ideas emerge when we allow ourselves time to think about imaginative possibilities.

Verse for the Day: "Do not neglect the gift that is in you" (1 Tim 4:14).

REPORTEDLY, THE 3M COMPANY strives to encourage its employees to be inventive and creative, and to explore ideas for developing new products. One of the ways the company does this is to give its research department time at work to spend on a pet project, something that isn't a part of their regular workload. By giving employees the oportunity to think outside the parameters of how things are always done, some innovative products have met success in the marketplace. One example has been the widely used Post-It-Note.

The thought occurred to Art Fry, a scientist at 3M, to put to use a certain adhesive a colleague had developed. The adhesive hadn't stuck very well, and so 3M had rejected it. Fry, however, discovered that it could serve a very practical purpose.

Each week Fry sang in the church choir and placed little slips of paper in his hymn book to mark the music selections. These slips of paper often would fall out of the book and flutter to the ground. One day, during his free time at work, Fry decided to try a little experiment. Taking some of the "useless" adhesive, he applied it to the back of a piece of paper. He tried it out as a bookmark and found that it did the trick. It stayed where it was supposed to and then could be removed without leaving a mark or tear in the page. The rest is history, for today Post-It-Notes are one of 3M's most successful office products.

We never know when times of creative thinking or activity will produce an idea that will catch on. And while to some, taking time to tinker and ponder may seem a waste of time, we can keep in mind that naysayers have often failed to see the significance and value of good things. For example: Lord Kelvin, Royal Society president from 1897 to 1899, reportedly commented, "Radio has no future" and "Heavier-than-air flying machines are impossible." In addition, in 1865, the *Boston Post* asserted, "Well-informed people know it is impossible to transmit the voice over wires and that were it possible to do so, the thing would be of no practical value."

The success of the radio, airplane, and telephone reminds us that time spent thinking, developing ideas, and creating has the potential to change the way we live, hopefully making our world a better place.

Prayer: As I spend time to think creatively, God, open my eyes to new ideas that will benefit others.

* * * *

SHEDDING FEAR, SHARING IDEAS

**Boldly expressing our ideas
allows others to help us explore them.**

*Verse for the Day: "The righteous are
as bold as a lion"* (Prov 28:1).

AS A NEW EMPLOYEE, I attended my first department's brainstorming meeting, and it loomed ominously in my mind. How could I share my ideas with these people? I was new. I didn't even know the rules yet. What if everyone just stared at me with that "Are you insane?" look when I offered my input.

All too soon the day of the meeting arrived, and before I knew it, I was sitting in circle of coworkers and that horrible moment came when it was my turn to toss out an idea. With my pulse racing, my palms sweating, and my stomach churning, I blurted my first contribution. Much to my relief, it was simply written down with the others, and no one seemed to be rolling their eyes.

I felt as if I'd just pulled the trigger in a game of Russian roulette. I had been lucky this time to find the chamber empty. But next time . . . ? I realized that this was not roulette at all. We were all working toward the same goal, and the more ideas, and the wider the variety of them, so much the better!

It's true that if I hadn't been forced to speak up that day, I likely never would have. And I suspect there are many people who keep their thoughts and dreams a secret, as I am prone to do. So what is it that keeps us from moving our ideas out of our heads and into the arena of exploration? In a word, fear. And what is it we're so afraid of when it comes to sharing our ideas? In another word, rejection. We fear that if we unveil our ideas and they are laughed at or rejected, then we are being rejected as well.

I learned something valuable in that brainstorming group several years ago: My value as a person will never be based on the value of my ideas. Some of my ideas were useful, and others never received a second thought, but even if every one of my suggestions was eventually shot down, I was no less a person for it.

Of course, it helps to have a place where we feel safe venturing to open up our ideas to honest scrutiny. Yet even at that, it takes boldness on our part to make the first step and conquer fear. For as fear is the enemy of exploration, boldness is the enemy of fear.

So what ideas are floating around in your mind that remain unexplored? With whom might you feel safe casting them out for discussion? Remembering that you are valuable regardless of how your ideas pan out, why not begin exploring their possibilities? Who knows, one of them might end up making a positive difference in the world. It's certainly worth a try.

Prayer: God, grant me boldness to explore the ideas in my mind and the dreams in my heart.

*   *   *   *

SELF-WORTH
I'M UNIQUELY MADE

. . . .

I HAVE A UNIQUE PERSPECTIVE
I have the privilege of seeing life
as no one else will ever see it.

*Verse for the Day: "I praise you, for I am
fearfully and wonderfully made"* (Psa 139:14).

WHEN I WAS A YOUNGSTER, my school teacher instructed my class to catch snowflakes on a piece of black paper. In this way she reminded us that no two flakes are ever exactly alike. "Each one is unique," she told us. "Each one is beautiful." I wondered how she could know if she hadn't compared them all—especially with all the snow that falls in Alaska. But I decided to take her word for it.

Just as each snowflake is unique, so are we—a fact that I have come to understand more and more as I have grown older. In addition, this snowflake analogy has made me aware of something else. Each time I get a glimpse of an individual snowflake on my sleeve or mitten, the thought strikes me that I, only I, have ever had the chance to see that particular design of snow crystals. It's a small but unique personal privilege.

Similarly, I have the unique privilege of viewing life through my particular set of lenses. One of our true claims to fame as humans is that we bring a one-of-a-kind perspective into the world, and by it, we enrich all who come in contact with us. It's a gift from our Creator, made more beautiful as we accept it with wonder.

Prayer: God, help me realize and appreciate the uniqueness of the special "window" through which I view life.

* * * *

MADE THIS WAY ON PURPOSE
You have been made with unique strengths for a unique purpose.

Verse for the Day: "The Lord will fulfill his purpose for me; your steadfast love, O Lord, endures forever. Do not forsake the work of your hands" (Psa 138:8).

ONE OF AESOP'S FABLES is about a reed and an olive tree. Both claimed to possess the ability to withstand the most adverse weather conditions. The olive tree, however, believed the reed was the weaker of the two. After all, even the slightest breeze could bend the little reed and make it sway to and fro. To this criticism, the reed answered not a word.

Later, when a fierce windstorm raged, the olive tree mustered all of its strength and took its stand against the powerful storm. Though very valiant, the olive tree's effort was unsuccessful, for the ferocious winds broke many of its branches and limbs. Meanwhile, the flexible reed rode out the blasts by bowing with each gust and remained unhurt throughout the powerful storm.

There are things about ourselves that we can't change—our basic personality, our physical features, our family tree, and so on. These things are part of what has contributed to making us who we are. Our inherited features, combined with our life experiences and other influences, have helped build our unique strengths and prepare us to fulfill our unique purpose on earth.

It's true that other people—and sometimes even we ourselves—may not always understand or appreciate the way our Creator has made us. Perhaps it is not until the wind of some adversity begins to stir that our unique strengths are suddenly called upon. Then all at once, when we are standing while others cannot and they turn to us for help, we finally see that it has all been for a reason, that God made us this way on purpose, and that purpose is exceedingly good.

Prayer: God, your purpose for my life, even when it is not evident, is good. Thank you for making me the way you have.

THE BUILDER OF LIVES
My life is a work of God's artistry.

Verse for the Day: "For we are what he has made us, created in Christ Jesus for good works, which God prepared beforehand to be our way of life" (Eph 2:10).

HAMMERS ARE POUNDING and electric saws are screaming while the house next door gets ever closer to completion. Five months ago, it was merely a cement foundation awkwardly sticking out of the earth. Today, there is no mistaking that it is a house that soon will be inhabited by a family—my new neighbors.

When we are young, we're a lot like that foundation—little more than an indication that a life is underway. As God continues his work, however, using the tools of experiences and people to build the structure of our life, we begin to have more and more of a sense that we are a special building in progress—the work of God himself.

When at last we reach maturity, there is no mistaking that God has been at work carefully crafting our life, building it up as a place of habitation—not only a place for our own enjoyment but also a place where our family and friends find comfort and shelter. Most significantly, the designer and builder himself responds readily to our invitation to fill the rooms of our life with the warmth and love only his presence can bring.

Prayer: God, your excellent workmanship is evident in the building of my life.

٭ ٭ ٭

MADE TO BE VALUED

The true indicator of our value lies in the price God was willing to pay for our lives.

Verse for the Day: "Wonderful are your works; that I know very well" (Psa 139:14).

ETERNITY MAGAZINE ONCE RELATED an incident in which a sidewalk flower vendor was wracking his brain for a way to increase sales. Suddenly the idea came into his mind to post a sign that read: Buy a gardenia: it will make you feel important all day long!

That little notice turned out to be just the ticket, boosting sales almost immediately.

We all have a need to feel valued. The sidewalk flower vendor discovered the power of this need when his sales pitch hit a chord with passersby. God created us with innate value, and on some level, we know it. But sometimes the words and actions of others make us feel as if we have little value. At times when we begin to doubt our value, God wants us to remember that he has established a standard for our worth.

While God is absolutely pure, he did not wash his hands of us once we fell short of his perfect standard. Knowing that the just penalty for our sin is death, God stepped in and paid the penalty for us in a great act of love and sacrifice. He offered his Son to be the one to die in our place. In doing this, God not only proved the greatness of his love for us but also established our value to him.

As we try to grasp the significance of what God has done for us, we may ask ourselves, "For what would I be willing to give the life of my son or daughter?" Is there anything valuable enough for such a sacrifice? God demonstrated that we were of such value to him.

A gardenia might make us feel important for a day, but taking to heart all God was willing to give up to free us from our moral debt and to give us eternal life with him will change our sense of personal value forever.

Prayer: God, I am your valued creation, and I rejoice in your love for me.

* * * *

MORE THAN THE SUM OF OUR PARTS

My mortal body is merely the container for the special person inside.

Verse for the Day: "For it was you who formed my inward parts" (Psa 139:13).

"YOUR NOSE IS really big," a junior high classmate of mine once observed. "And it's got a big hump in the middle."

As if I didn't know. In those self-conscious years of growing into my nose (which I'm not sure I ever quite did), I heard all kinds of opinions about its size and shape. "It makes a good witch's nose" and "It looks kind of like my basset hound's" were among the comments about my infamous facial appendage.

Many make the transition into adulthood with impressions about ourselves handed to us by our peers of yesteryear. Somehow their epithets stick in our subconscious, making us feel as if we'll always be a little less desirable and flawed in everyone else's estimation.

Of course, time mercifully diminishes the impact of youth's unkind remarks, and we move on to find that there's more to life than a perfect face or physique. Nevertheless, a specter of the insecurity sometimes remains, coming to haunt us whenever we encounter someone we feel is more valuable than we are because of that person's appearance. At such times, our unique beauty becomes buried in a sudden avalanche of self-loathing. Indeed, the light of our specialness is extinguished, not because of the other person's superior worth, but because we have forgotten our own worth and what it is really based on.

Our bodies, incredible as they are, are mere casings for the person within. Our worth is based, not on the body, though many mistakenly believe so, but wholly on its invaluable contents. God carefully placed in each of us the capacity to relate to him in an entirely unique way. He has no other creature who can bring what we can to a relationship with him, as well as to relationships with others. Therein will always lie the beauty of our existence and our true worth.

Prayer: Today, God, help me realize the great value of the person inside my body.

* * * *

I'm Exceptionally Gifted

* * * *

Giving Our Giftedness to the World

Sharing our gifts and abilities with others is a present benefit and a future blessing.

Verse for the Day: "They refreshed my spirit as well as yours. So give recognition to such persons" (1 Cor 16:18).

THE CIVIL WAR WAS nearing its conclusion when a slave girl named Mary gave birth to a baby she named George. A weak and frail infant, George wasn't expected to live. Then, tragically, the baby was separated from his mother when they were abducted from the Carver farm and each sold to a different man.

Moses Carver—the legal owner of Mary and George—had a friend who searched diligently for the two, but he was able to locate only George, whom he brought back. With Mary gone and George's father having died in a farm accident, Moses and Susan Carver, who were childless, raised George until he was about 10 or 12 years old.

It was evident at an early age that George Washington Carver had a exceptional love for nature and an insatiable thirst for knowledge. He once told Susan Carver that he wanted to know all there was to know about everything. He later wrote, "When just a mere tot, my very soul thirsted for an education. I literally lived in the woods. I wanted to know every strange stone, flower, insect, bird, or beast."

After acquiring a high school diploma in his late twenties, George Washington Carver received a B.S. degree in agriculture from Iowa State Agricultural College. After earning his Master of Science degree, Carver became a member of the faculty of Tuskegee Institute in Alabama.

Carver became one of the country's most respected agriculturists. When southern farmers had depleted their soil from growing only cotton without rotating their crops, Carver suggested that they begin crop rotation, planting peanuts and sweet potatoes to help enrich the worn-out soil.

When the farmers continued to lose money after planting the new crops, Carver prayed that God would help him discover new uses for peanuts and sweet potatoes. Carver went on to discover 300 marketable products made from the peanut, including soap, rubber, shampoo, mayonnaise, cheese, and axle grease. The sweet potato, Carver discovered, had 118 uses, some of which include starch, vinegar, and molasses.

As George Washington Carver persevered through poverty and prejudice to share his giftedness with the world, he gained the well-deserved respect and admiration of his contemporaries and a place in history as one who will receive admiration and gratitude for generations to come.

Prayer: Dear God, as I share the exceptional gifts and abilities you have entrusted to me, may others be uniquely enriched and blessed.

* * * *

HONORING GOD WITH OUR GIFTEDNESS
We honor God when we use our gifts and talents in positive ways.

~⊗~

Verse for the Day: "Well done, good and trustworthy slave; you have been trustworthy in a few things, I will put you in charge of many things" (Matt 25:21).

DWIGHT MOODY WAS a hard worker from the time he was a boy. When he turned 17, he headed to Boston, where his uncle owned a shoe store. There he put in many hours as a sales clerk for his uncle. Then, at age 18, a Sunday school teacher challenged Moody to commit his life to living in a way that would honor God. This challenge had a profound impact on the young shoe clerk, and he began to think more and more about how he might live more purposefully.

The next year, Moody moved to Chicago with his sights set on earning $100,000. By the time he was 23, the young entrepreneur was well on his way to attaining his goal. His deepening faith, however, was causing him to lose interest in material things, and his attention was increasingly drawn to the needs of the poverty-stricken European immigrants living in the city. It wasn't long until Moody was totally immersed in his passion for serving others.

He used lecture halls and theaters to address the spiritual needs of the people he was helping, and he was able to effectively communicate the love and grace of God to multitudes, regardless of their religious background. People flocked to hear him talk, and his popularity grew rapidly. Presidents Lincoln and Grant both attended his famous revival services.

Moody's zeal for ministry was not limited to preaching and teaching. His heart for the welfare of others led him to open two educational facilities, which are still in operation today: the Northfield school for boys and girls, and the Chicago Evangelism Society, later renamed Moody Bible Institute. Publishing was another of the avenues of ministry in which Moody invested himself. Moody Publishing still bears his name.

In his lifetime, Moody traveled hundreds of thousands of miles to speak to millions of people about God's love, and he led hundreds of thousands, if not millions, to a personal faith in God. Moody was, without question, one of history's most gifted and influential ministers, and using his abilities to give God his best efforts characterized his life.

Prayer: God, let my gifts and talents bless others and bring praise to you.

▪ ▪ ▪ ▪

SHARING OUR GIFTEDNESS
We enrich ourselves and others when we share our giftedness.

～⊚～

Verse for the Day: "Like good stewards of the manifold grace of God, serve one another with whatever gift each of you has received" (1 Pet 4:10).

VIENNA'S MUSEUM OF FINE ARTS once had the privilege of being offered the free services of an interesting elderly man, whom the museum staff affectionately dubbed "The Pharaoh." As the story goes, it was over a span of 30 years that he would wait at the museum's entrance and volunteer to take visitors through the many exhibits, particularly explaining Egyptian art in great detail.

Most visitors thought he was employed by the museum, but he had no official connection with it. Experts and professors of Egyptology, however, were amazed at his knowledge and would seek him out for information about things that baffled them. It wasn't until "The Pharaoh" passed away that an interesting bit of truth about his life was revealed; never once had he visited the place he knew so much about.

This brief account gives a glimpse into the life of a man who was eager to share his gift of knowledge with the world. His passion for Egyptian art and history, no doubt, had fed his desire to learn all that he could about it. Despite the fact that he never had the privilege of touring the Great Pyramids or of participating in archeological digs, he was an expert in his field of study. Yet he was not satisfied just to be a gifted historian—to merely have the expertise. His joy was not complete unless he could give his gift away to others, and he did this free of charge.

Though some considered him eccentric, the man they called "The Pharaoh" was no fool. He lived his life enjoying his passion and sharing the intangible riches of his gift with others.

Prayer: God, grant me opportunities to enrich those around me with the abilities you have placed within me.

* * * *

I HAVE A SPECIAL ROLE

* * * *

SENIORS DESPERATELY NEEDED

Seniors play a vital role in maintaining a whole and healthy society.

Verse for the Day: "Tell the older men to be . . . sound in faith, in love, and in endurance" (Titus 2:2).

CERTAINLY BEING OLD IS a matter of perspective, as Lillian Carter, the mother of former President Carter, reminded the public at age 85 when she said, "Sure, I'm for helping the elderly. I'm going to be old myself one day."

Yet old age is also a reality—a blessed reality that exists in our society as we look out at a topsy-turvy world. The British poet Samuel T. Coleridge said it well: "I have often thought what a melancholy world this would be without children, and what an inhuman world without the aged."

The "grandparents" of each generation bring an indispensable gentleness to life along with a certain steadiness. The comfort and reassurance these qualities bring to a community are what the young, and especially children, so desperately need as they face an often harsh and uncaring world.

Gentleness and stability are strengths that run deep and wide. They are but two of the many refreshing positives that seniors bring to a culture that has become parched by negative influences. Like a drink of cool water in the desert, seniors are desperately needed today...and tomorrow...and the next day—and always.

Prayer: As the younger generations need what my generation brings to life, God, let me be there for them.

◊ ◊ ◊ ◊

COMPLETING THE PICTURE
The big picture is not complete without us in it.

Verse for the Day: "Indeed, the body does not consist of one member but of many....But as it is, God arranged the members in the body, each one of them, as he chose" (1 Cor 12:14, 18).

WHENEVER EITHER BARB or Thelma acquired a new jigsaw puzzle, they would make plans to get together and tackle the thousand-or-more-piece monster. Inevitably, when all the available pieces had been put in place, there would be one piece missing. Aha! There was a caper afoot, but it was certainly no mystery. Thelma's son Andy made a habit of surreptitiously swiping one piece and hiding it. That way, he would have the distinct pleasure of completing the picture.

Of course, there might be 1,499 pieces all exactly where they belonged, but no one considered the puzzle complete as long as there was that glaring hole where the final piece should fit. In unison, the women would call Andy's name, and he would come smiling into the room, reach into his pocket, and pull out The Piece. As he popped it handily into its obvious place, the sense of completeness was satisfying.

The analogy to our lives may seem obvious, but often we don't see ourselves as being the piece without which the picture would be incomplete. We may look around and see that the 1,499 pieces seem well and good enough and that we aren't really that important in the scheme of things. What we may forget, however, is that when the spot we were cut out to fill is empty, the picture is left with an even greater sense of incompleteness than if 200 pieces were missing.

It's not until we are functioning, using our God-given gifts to complete the big picture, that everyone begins to benefit from the satisfaction such wholeness brings. Let it be your distinct pleasure to always fill your special place—a place only you can fit into to make things as they should be.

Prayer: God, I long to fill my special place as an essential part of your body of believers.

* * * *

Book-Learnin' Isn't Everything

Education comes in many forms, helping equip us for our special role in life.

Verse for the Day: "They are well instructed; their God teaches them" (Isa 28:26).

CARL OFTEN LAMENTS that he never had a post-high-school education. From his perspective, because he doesn't have a college degree, his skill and opportunities have been somewhat limited.

One of Carl's college-educated friends, however, sees things differently where Carl is concerned. Although Carl's high level of creativity and ingenuity in the area of mechanical engineering doesn't have the credentials of a university behind it, Carl has secured and marketed a number of patents for some large machinery. Carl's knowledge of farm equipment and his experience operating other big machines have given him an education he couldn't have learned in a mere textbook full of theory. Carl's friend even speculates that the influences of a formal education might have curtailed Carl's creativity. Meanwhile, several other innovations float around in Carl's mind, waiting to materialize as he finds time.

While there's much to be said for formal training (we're all more comfortable knowing our physicians received their education from reputable institutions), it's certainly not the only effective means for being equipped for a special role in life. There's much to know about life that cannot be imparted in the classroom or from a textbook. There are secrets of nature, lessons of experience, and skills that can be learned only from observation and practice.

Our roles are unique and varied. As individuals each of us has received our education by different means, in different places, and at different times. Whether the training be "formal" or "informal" doesn't really matter if it has equipped us to do our part in helping make the world go round.

Prayer: Assist me, God, as I put to good use the training I've received in the school of life.

❧ ❧ ❧ ❧

SUCCESS
CELEBRATING MY SUCCESSES

* * * *

CELEBRATING TRUE SUCCESS

As we enjoy a successful life, we can celebrate from deep within our souls.

Verse for the Day: "Therefore walk in the way of the good, and keep to the paths of the just. For the upright will abide in the land, and the innocent will remain in it" (Prov 2:20–21).

*T*HE WORD SUCCESS has many different definitions because people have different ideas about what it means to be successful.

Society, as a whole, points to the rich and famous, declaring, "Now, these are the really successful people!" And as we look at their elegant homes, their tailor-made clothes, the dream cars they drive, and the seeming limitlessness of their freedoms, we may be tempted to think that our lives really aren't successful in any way that counts. There is, however, a kind of success—real success—that is far out of the reach of the almighty dollar.

The perspective of years makes clear this distinction between superficial and true success. It understands the questions Jesus put forth: "What will it profit them if they gain the whole world but forfeit their life? Or what will they give in return for their life?" (Matt 16:26). The precious gift of life is an opportunity to discover all that makes existence meaningful—the things for which we were meant to live. Thus it is only out of these things that the soul enjoys the celebration of its valued purpose.

In the Bible, God outlines the formula for a successful life journey: "To do justly, and to love kindness, and to walk humbly with your God" (Mic 6:8). As we consider this biblical instruction, we can write out our personal definition of success, including what has made our life successful in God's eyes and what makes our days full and meaningful. As we realize all of the success we have enjoyed and are yet enjoying, we can celebrate from deep within our souls.

Prayer: God, today I celebrate within my heart the success of fullness and meaning you grant me as I journey through life.

* * * *

CELEBRATING PERSONAL VICTORY

Personal victories, no matter how large or small, are worth celebrating.

Verse for the Day: "A desire realized is sweet to the soul" (Prov 13:19).

DID YOU KNOW that Edward Gibbon worked for 20 years on his historical work *Decline and Fall of the Roman Empire*? That George Bancroft put in 26 years writing his *History of the United States*? And how about Noah Webster, who spent 36 years on his dictionary?

"The secret of success," noted British politician and author Benjamin Disraeli, "is constancy of purpose."

Undoubtedly!

When we've put forth our best effort and have produced our best work, our personal successes are no less glorious than those mentioned above. They may not be world renown, but they are victories to be savored and worthy of celebration.

Have you set and met a personal goal recently? Have you finished a project that you had been working on for a long time? Have you kept at something when you felt like giving up? Have you overcome a fear or a habit that you thought you never could?

What are your personal victories?

Celebrate them! Tell a friend. Treat yourself to something special. Acknowledge that you have done something well. Look in the mirror, flash a victory smile, and say, "I did it!"

Prayer: God, today I celebrate the victory you have granted and the strength you've provided so that I could persevere.

. . . .

AN INVENTORY OF SUCCESSES

Taking inventory of my successes gives me an opportunity to celebrate them.

Verse for the Day: "The boundary lines have fallen for me in pleasant places; I have a goodly heritage" (Psa 16:6).

*F*OR A TIME, I WORKED AS a clerk in an aerospace machine shop. It was a quarterly practice for the company to halt work every few months and take an inventory. In essence, it was a way to step back and see just how far we'd come.

In the Verse for the Day the psalmist David was looking over his life—taking a personal inventory of sorts—and recognizing just how good he had it. Similarly, as we occasionally pause to look over our lives, we can take a little inventory of our successes and then make an effort to celebrate them.

If you were to inventory your successes, what would top your list? Children and grandchildren? Other special relationships? Educational triumphs? Overcoming particular difficulties or obstacles? The attainment of good character? An inventory takes some time. Pause and give yourself a chance to get a good "count."

Then celebrate. Celebrate your successes, big and small. Celebration can include thanking and praising God. It might involve calling children or grandchildren and telling them that we count them among our highest achievements. Perhaps you've never framed a diploma or an award you've earned. Even reading your spouse's old love letters can be a celebration of the success of your relationship together.

However you choose to celebrate, enjoy counting and rejoicing in the glorious moments you have had thus far along life's way.

Prayer: The successes you've granted me, dear God, have been sweet, and I praise you for them.

HELPING OTHERS SUCCEED

∗ ∗ ∗ ∗

ENCOURAGING EXCELLENCE

When we lovingly challenge others to improve, we help them move toward success.

Verse for the Day: "Give instruction to the wise, and they will become wiser still; teach the righteous and they will gain in learning" (Prov 9:9).

A YOUNG ARTIST took his painting of the Last Supper to the great Russian writer Leo Tolstoy. He wanted to get the novelist's impression of his work. Tolstoy gazed at the painting for several moments before stating, "You do not love him."

"Why, that's the Lord Jesus Christ!" the artist exclaimed.

"I know," said Tolstoy, "but you do not love him. If you loved him more, you would paint him better."

Such direct criticism! Yet was Tolstoy's remark aimed at tearing down the artist's confidence? Of course not. Tolstoy knew that the success the young painter craved would be achieved only through his continual striving for excellence. Therefore, when Tolstoy was asked for his opinion, he spoke the truth from a heart of love.

As those who admire our perspective come to us for feedback and advice, they deserve not only our kindness but also our honesty. When we challenge them (within the context of our love for them) to achieve excellence, we give them a unique gift. For many may flatter and give the easy word of praise, and still others will criticize in a mean-spirited way, but few will care and dare to give the word of loving, constructive criticism. If we so choose, we can be that rare individual, urging excellence and helping others toward success.

Prayer: God, give me your loving insight when offering the kind of encouragement that comes in the form of constructive criticism.

* * * *

ACTS OF SELF-SACRIFICE

When we give of ourselves to help others achieve success, it is the noblest of sacrifices.

Verse for the Day: "For God so loved the world that he gave his only Son, so that everyone who believes in him... may have eternal life" (John 3:16).

BEFORE THE USE OF FIREARMS the Austrians and the Swiss were at war with each other. At the battle of Sempach, the Austrian army greatly outnumbered the Swiss army. Thus the Austrians could launch an impenetrable hail of spears, repelling any Swiss attack.

Nevertheless, Arnold Winkelried rallied the Swiss soldiers in his company by encouraging them to follow him into battle. He assured them that he would open a way to victory. Charging the Austrian front, Winkelried courageously deflected as many spears as he could reach with his arms. Numerous spears, however, pierced his body, and he crumpled to the ground and died. Still, his act of sacrifice had created enough of an opening to allow other Swiss soldiers to press through the Austrian line and win the battle.

There are many such stories of personal sacrifice, and each one is moving in its own way. Indeed, the voluntary forfeit of one's life for the sake of others is the deepest kind of commitment to the success of another human being.

Not all acts of self-sacrifice, however, are to the death. Many of us can look back and recall how our parents sacrificed to give us our clothes, our meals, our education, and other provisions. We may recall how, as parents, we have done the same for our children. At times, we may have sacrificed our time, our salary level, our chances for prestige and power to help someone else achieve their goals and dreams.

Such are the living sacrifices that loudly proclaim our genuine love and concern for others above ourselves though they be ever so quietly given. They are noble, and they are precious in the sight of God, who knows what it feels like to give up something precious to make a way for others to succeed.

Prayer: God, may the sacrifices I make honor you and may they bear the fruit of true success in the lives of others.

. . . .

BEING AN AGENT OF SUCCESS

Our encouragement has the power to help others succeed.

Verse for the Day: "Do not withhold good . . . when it is in your power to do it" (Prov 3:27).

"WHAT A SIMPLETON!" Chuck chided himself. "A child could get this piece of music right, but I just keep making the same mistakes over and over." Chuck was learning to play the bass guitar, and while he enjoyed practicing with his friends in the band, he felt frustrated at his inability to catch on more quickly.

In the middle of Chuck's struggle, however, there was Nate, the band's drummer and a talented musician. Nate would take time to go over difficult rhythms and sections of music with Chuck so that he could get them right. "Good job, tonight, Chuck," Nate would always say when the rehearsal was over, maybe even noting some aspect of improvement in Chuck's playing.

At first, Chuck had a hard time accepting Nate's encouragement. Later in the week, however, as he practiced playing, Nate's words would come back to him, providing him with much-needed inspiration to keep working.

Encouragers are agents of success. As we struggle, their cheers for us often keep us from pulling out of the race too soon. Their belief in our potential helps us believe in ourselves. Without encouragers, many victories would go unclaimed.

We can be agents for the success of others simply by encouraging them to continue reaching for their goals, to never give up, and to claim their victory. As we lift other souls along our way, their victories will become our own.

Prayer: God, may I be an agent of success in the lives of others today.

*   *   *   *

WISDOM
LEARNING FROM ONE'S EXPERIENCES

. . . .

LEARNING ABOUT GOD THROUGH EXPERIENCE

We learn about God's character by experiencing his loving presence in our lives.

Verse for the Day: "O taste and see that the Lord is good; happy are those who take refuge in him" (Psa 34:8).

*A*S OUR EXPERIENCES FILL the pages of our lives, our perspective on God often changes. Through life's ups and downs we may come to an eventual trust that God has a good plan and purpose for us. Or we may come to believe that he is cruel and arbitrary while we struggle to come to terms with disappointment, loss, or tragedy. How we choose to interpret our experiences is a large part of the development of our faith.

Nevertheless, regardless of the way we interpret our experiences, one thing is certain: God's character does not change. As the story of our lives is written, God seeks to inscribe one supreme truth on our hearts: his unfailing love for us. God literally longs to be in close relationship with us and to care for us as only he can.

Although we live in a world that contains evil and pain, God will guide us through this world and will never leave us alone in it. Experiencing his presence in this way will change our lives forever.

Prayer: God, your love is life-changing, and I long to experience it in ever-deepening ways.

GAINING WISDOM FROM MISTAKES

Our mistakes can have redeeming value when we gain wisdom from them.

Verse for the Day: "You desire truth in the inward being; therefore teach me wisdom in my secret heart" (Psa 51:6).

THE VERSE FOR THE DAY comes from King David's psalm to God in which he confessed his moral failure—that is, his adulterous relationship with Bathsheba followed by his plot to murder her husband. The consequences of his sins filled his heart with anguish, and yet in his sincere confession David found relief and forgiveness. Moreover, he gained an understanding of the destructive nature of wickedness from his experience. The "school of hard knocks," painful as it was, had increased the king's wisdom substantially.

Oscar Wilde, a nineteenth-century Irish writer, asserted, "To deny one's own experiences is to put a lie into the lips of one's own life. It is no less than a denial of the soul." Along these same lines, eighteenth-century English satirist Jonathan Swift said, "A man should never be ashamed to own he has been in the wrong, which is but saying, in other words, that he is wiser today than he was yesterday."

Failure can be painful, and its consequences sometimes monumental. Yet on disappointment's side of experience, there is a grace we can obtain if we are willing to receive it. That grace is a gift called "wisdom"—the understanding we can gain from the bumps and bruises of experience.

Those who have lived many years and who have not been too proud to accept the grace of learning from their mistakes are the ones who have turned the inevitability of human shortcomings into the advantageous ways of wisdom.

Prayer: Gracious God, thank you for the grace of wisdom that has come to me from my mistakes.

❧ ❧ ❧ ❧

THE VOICE OF EXPERIENCE

Our experiences often qualify us to offer wisdom to those who are coming along behind us.

Verse for the Day: "*Wisdom is at home in the mind of one who has understanding*" (Prov 14:33).

SIMON BOLIVAR BUCKNER, a famous American general, enjoyed relating a conversation between a wise older gentleman and a younger man.

"How does it come you're so wise?" asked the younger.

"Because," the older gentleman replied, "I've got good judgment. Good judgment comes from experience, and experience—well, that comes from poor judgment!"

The voice of experience. It's a voice worth listening to. Experience means one has been there before, knows the lay of the land, and can give some helpful navigating tips to those who are heading in that direction.

Today, you are the voice of experience for many who are starting out into territory you know well. Have you reflected on lessons you've learned from your experiences? Have you chronicled any of these in a journal? Do you talk about experiences you've had so younger folks can understand you've "been there, done that"?

Be the voice of experience for those who are farther back on the trail. Let your children and grandchildren know what you know. Don't be afraid to talk about the past. Sure, times change, but people don't, and we all face uncertainty and the same general difficulties in life. Speak up. You may just be able to make the journey a little easier, the way a little clearer for someone else, for you are the much-needed voice of experience.

Prayer: My experiences, God, have given me wisdom; grant me the voice to pass them along to those coming after me.

᛭ ᛭ ᛭

NOTING WISDOM IN OTHERS

᛭ ᛭ ᛭

THE BENEFITS OF WISE FRIENDS

Trusted friends are an excellent source of wise counsel.

Verse for the Day: "The righteous gives good advice to friends" (Prov 12:26).

PROFESSIONAL ADVICE can be costly. Consider the following story:

At a social gathering a counselor was finally able to disengage herself from someone who knew of her profession and wanted some advice. After sitting down at her table with a group of acquaintances, she related her encounter and asked, "Do you think I should charge her for my time?"

"Why not?" a financial consultant replied.

"Really?" she asked.

"Sure," she said. "By listening to her, you gave her some of your time."

When the counselor arrived at her office the following day, she instructed her administrative assistant to bill the woman from the party. She then discovered a letter from the financial consultant. It indicated that she owed $100 for professional advice received.

Fortunately, not all the advice we seek is of a professional nature. In fact, when we're looking for guidance or insight on a particular issue we're facing—even one that ultimately requires a professional opinion—we most often turn first to a trusted friend.

Wise friends who have our best interest at heart take the time to consider our situation carefully with us. They pass along useful information and experiences to help us as we weigh decisions. They counsel us with love, not with professional indifference. They make it their business to make sure we're on a safe path.

When we're at a loss for what to do, or if we're facing a tough call, it's good to know we have a source of wisdom that is based in love for us and a deep commitment to our well-being. Yes, costly professional counsel is sometimes necessary, but the wise counsel of trusted friends is indispensable and absolutely priceless.

Prayer: The wellspring of wisdom from loving friends, God, is such a help and a comfort when I need it.

* * * *

WISDOM OF THE AGES
Pondering ancient wisdom can help us strengthen our own wisdom.

Verse for the Day: "For ask now about former ages, long before your own" (Deut 4:32).

HERE ARE SOME OF NUGGETS of wisdom from six philosophers of ancient Greece:

Solon of Athens—"Know yourself." Pittacos of Mitylene—"Make the most of each moment." Bias of Priene—"Most people are wicked." Cleobulos of Lindos—"Don't be an extremist." Periander of Corinth—"Hard work attains any goal." Chile of Sparta—"Ponder the consequences."

As you read these sayings, how does each strike you? As false? As true in only one sense? As absolutely true? Why? How might you amend some of these to better reflect what you have come to understand about life?

As we consider the philosophies and beliefs of others, they challenge us to develop our own beliefs, to understand them better, and to be stronger in them. It's good to know that we don't need to fear the beliefs of others, for truth can always stand on its own. And when we diligently seek truth's infallible wisdom, we will find it. That's a promise God himself has given us.

Prayer: God, I rejoice in knowing that you are the truth and that all truth belongs to you.

. . . .

A SHORTCUT TO WISDOM
Observing the lives of others can be a shortcut to wisdom.

～◯～

Verse for the Day: "The clever see danger and hide; but the simple go on, and suffer for it" (Prov 27:12).

BETTY IS IN HER SEVENTIES and sharp as a tack. She stays up on all of the current events news. She also keeps up with the latest scams that target elderly people. Having read magazine articles and watched television exposés about devious crooks who have devastated the bank accounts of countless seniors, she has learned from their experiences to be wary.

Betty's wisdom has taught her not to do business with people or companies who phone or knock at her door and promise something if she'll just pay that amount or send in a check for so much money. She knows that she may sometimes be passing up legitimate deals, but she also knows that if they're not for real, she won't have to learn the hard way.

Learning from the experiences of others can be a shortcut to getting wisdom. When we see the benefits others gain from a certain course of action or witness a painful lesson another person has endured, we can glean knowledge from the ups and downs of these fellow travelers and gain insights for our own journey as we walk the path of life.

Prayer: Dear God, as I seek a wise path for me, show me the shortcuts that others reveal to me through their experiences.

*   *   *   *

Guided and Protected by Wisdom

. . . .

That Inner Voice
We do well when we listen to wisdom's
whispers from within.

*Verse for the Day: "I bless the Lord who gives me counsel; in
the night also my heart instructs me"* (Psa 16:7).

HAVE YOU EVER HAD a strong urging that you
should or shouldn't do something and discover
later that your inclination was right on? I'm not talking
about mere hunches, but rather that sense of knowing
the right thing to do.

That is our inner voice of wisdom, and it is usually
informed by our experience—our sense of right and
wrong—and God's own Spirit who guides our steps.
We can be certain that when we hear it speaking, it is in
our best interest that we listen and act without delay.

On one level, the inner voice may remind us that we
should go back into the house because we've left a stove
burner on. On another level, we may sense that though
we are tempted to pass along a tidbit of gossip, it would
be prudent not to speak. On a higher, more spiritual
level, we may feel a definite inner prompting to pray

for someone or to give someone a phone call, though the reasons aren't immediately evident to us.

Yet on whatever level we receive instruction from our inner voice, we can thank God who has given us the ability to discern its promptings, and thus to experience wisdom's guidance and protection.

Prayer: God, in your graciousness you provide wisdom for my protection and guidance through the still voice within.

* * * *

KEPT SAFE BY WISDOM
Wisdom is a heritage that provides protection from harm.

Verse for the Day: "Do not forsake [wisdom], and she will keep you; love her, and she will guard you" (Prov 4:6).

THE BOY STOOD PERFECTLY STILL, holding the board he had just lifted from the ground. His father, who was at a distance, called to him to hurry and bring the lumber. Instead of responding, however, the boy stayed where he was, holding the board vertically, with one end of it resting on the ground; he did not speak a word to his dad.

Because the father had taught his son to always respond whenever called, it was immediately obvious to the father that his son was in some sort of trouble. Hurrying toward the boy, the father heard an unmistakable rattling and realized that a poisonous snake lay coiled at his son's feet. Quickly bringing a shovel, the father severed the snake's head, saving his son from a potentially fatal rattlesnake bite.

The father's wisdom in training his son had paid off. Had the son not learned to answer when he was called, his father might have assumed that he was simply disobeying. Instead, the father was able to discern right away that his son needed help.

The boy in the story was my grandfather. He followed the wisdom of his father by teaching his children to respond at once to his call. This wisdom saved my dad's life when he was only three years old.

As the story goes, a team of horses pulling a sickle mower had run into a beehive. My grandfather had lost control of the horses, and they were headed toward my dad, who was playing alone nearby. In desperation, my grandfather called out instructions to his son. The little boy, though not fully realizing the danger he was in, responded promptly. Mere seconds later, my dad watched from atop a stump he had climbed, as the horses and mower passed directly over where he had been standing.

This same wisdom, handed down from my grandfather and great-grandfather, was part of the protection my siblings and I enjoyed while growing up. Today, my sister and brother have children who know that they must respond immediately when they are called.

As for myself, I'm certain that this heritage of wisdom has spared me from any number of bumps and bruises, as well as more serious accidents. And I wonder, how many more lives will be saved in generations to come because my grandparents were wise in this matter of training their children?

Prayer: Thank you, God, that my wisdom can offer protection to others as I pass it along.

* * * *

KNOWLEDGE NEEDS WISDOM

Our knowledge guided by wisdom protects us from pitfalls.

Verse for the Day: "Wisdom is better than weapons of war" (Eccl 9:18).

MAX BORN WAS a good friend of Albert Einstein. He also worked with the nuclear physicists Max Planck and Otto Hahn.

On German television prior to his death in January 1970, Born stated, "I'd be happier if we had scientists with less brains and more wisdom."

With the technology for nuclear power having been developed, it was quickly applied to the creation and use of nuclear weapons. No doubt, Born, at least in part, was referring to the fact that though the knowledge about nuclear energy had been discovered, it did not follow that it would be used wisely.

Even in our everyday lives, the need for wisdom to guide our knowledge is evident. We may have read a hundred books on a topic, but wisdom will always tell us to gain some understanding about a situation before we barge in with our wealth of knowledge, trying to fix things.

Just as truth needs love in order to be effective, so knowledge needs wisdom. Wisdom guides our knowledge and protects us from the sharp, dangerous side of mere intellect. Our Creator has endowed us with a wonderful gift: the mind. And we honor him when we acquire knowledge and then use that knowledge wisely.

Prayer: As I acquire knowledge, God, grant me wisdom that I will minimize its harm and maximize its usefulness to others.

*   *   *   *

PASSING WISDOM TO OTHERS

. . . .

WISDOM'S APPEAL

**Our actions can sometimes teach wisdom
more effectively than our words do.**

*Verse for the Day: "The integrity of the upright
guides them, but the crookedness of the treacherous
destroys them" (Prov 11:3).*

NINETEENTH-CENTURY PREACHER Charles Spurgeon
once said, "If a crooked stick is before you, you
need not explain how crooked it is. Lay a straight one
down by the side of it, and the work is well done."

Grandpa Jones was a man of few words, but his actions were powerfully loud. He led by example, not by
talk. When Gina was a girl, she used to want Grandpa
Jones to peel an apple for her before they sat down
together to watch *The Wonderful World of Disney* on
television.

One evening, Gina asked if she could try peeling
the apple. She'd never paid too much attention to
Grandpa's apple-peeling technique, but she liked how
he'd cut the peel in one long coil. She thought she'd
give it a try.

Handing Gina a paring knife and an apple, Grandpa Jones simply said, "Be careful, now," and let her go to work. But rather than leave her to her task, Grandpa Jones picked up his own apple, washed it, and pulled out another paring knife. As Gina started to peel her apple, she realized that she really didn't know how to do it the way her grandpa did. In fact, she'd already severed the coil she was trying to make.

When she looked over at his hands, she knew he was peeling more slowly than usual for her benefit. Rather than try to lecture Gina about the intricacies of his apple-peeling ritual, Grandpa simply, as Charles Spurgeon might describe it, laid his "straight stick" next to Gina's crooked one, and the work of passing along his wisdom was under way.

That was generally Grandpa Jones's style. He gave advice on occasion, but as a rule, he preferred to gently lead by example. And when grandchildren paid attention, they could gain a good deal of insight just by watching him.

Prayer: God, show me where I might lay down the straight stick of wisdom you've given me so that it might guide others.

* * * *

WISDOM TO LAUNCH A LIFE

My wisdom can guide the young as they start out in life.

Verse for the Day: "Hear, my child, and accept my words, that the years of your life may be many" (Prov 4:10).

IF IT WEREN'T FOR THE guidance and encouragement of the older and wiser ones in the lives of the young people entering the world of adulthood, each successive generation, in essence, would have to reinvent the wheel—that is, discover the principles of life through trial and error without any foresight.

What a huge advantage for the young person who shares a relationship with a loved and respected grandparent! That young person can maximize his or her life journey, stepping over many stumbling blocks and embracing key opportunities. Indeed, "someone who's been there" can impart the wisdom of a lifetime to a young adult.

Prayer: God, as the young adults I know and love are starting out in life, allow the wisdom I share with them to guide them and encourage them along the way.

❧ ❧ ❧ ❧

The Influence of Wisdom
The influence of my wisdom may be subtle,
but it has the power to be highly effective.

Verse for the Day: "*I am reminded of your sincere faith, a faith that lived first in your grandmother Lois and your mother Eunice and now, I am sure, lives in you*" (2 Tim 1:5).

A GUN-MANUFACTURING FACILITY demonstrated how a huge bar of steel could be set in motion by the persistent influence upon it of a very light object. Setting up the experiment, workers dangled a huge bar of steel vertically from a chain. Next to it, a silk thread hung with a cork attached to the end of it. The cork was made to swing and bump gently against the steel bar. For several minutes, nothing happened: The bar remained perfectly still. After ten minutes had passed, however, observers noticed an almost imperceptible shiver that seemed to run through the bar. At the 20-minute mark, the bar was clearly vibrating. When 30 minutes had passed, the cork had set the bar to swinging like the pendulum on a grandfather clock.

Sometimes we can feel as if the influence of our wisdom in the lives of our children and grandchildren is like a cork thumping uselessly against the massive weight of a steel bar. Our best-intended help and direction may seem no match for the other influences in their lives, such as popular culture, peers, and ego.

Parents and grandparents, however, have an advantage that most of the other influences don't. While other elements of persuasion may come and go in the lives of the younger generations, parents and grandparents can continue to be there, gently bumping up against the lives of their loved ones, reminding them of the things that are true and meaningful and wise. Given time, the influence of loving wisdom can put resistant lives in motion, possibly even changing a destiny or two.

Prayer: God, I'm grateful that I can be a steady influence in the lives of my children and grandchildren, imparting wisdom that can have a greater and greater impact over time.

*   *   *   *